Dedicated to my grandchildren,
Aibar, Aisultan and Mikaela Merei, ...
And my children Yerzhan and Zhibek, Yerlan and Madina,
Aidar and Umitgul.

Raushan is a wonderful person, soft lyric writer, friend of my family. She has something very-very closely related to my soul. Dear Raushan, by sharing my opinion as one of your dedicated readers, I feel that your poetry is just like a sunny day. It still hits me off even though my soul is unpoetic and more prosaic. Therefore, I warmly appreciate and feel very-very sympathetic toward your poetic creations!

Abdizhamil Nurpeisov – People's writer of Kazakhstan

The poetic creations of Raushan Burkitbayeva-Nukenova have enriched the Kazakh culture. They popularize Kazakh poetry, contribute to the development of friendship and ties between the states. Her works are included in school curriculum. They enhance and educate the younger generation on how to become patriots that also awakes the interest toward the history of our people.

Nurlan Orazalin – The President of the Writers' Union of Kazakhstan

Raushan is a glorious poet, precise lyricist and great housewife. I am captured by your romances that follow the best traditions of uniting East and West.

Nikolay Anastas'yev – Moscow, the Professor of Moscow State University

Her line is so free and loveful. Her word is reedy and soft. Her poems are smooth and in tune to Russian muse. I think that Raushan's creativity is like a key to comprehend the East, its solid traditions, colors, tunes and flavors.

Giorgiy Pryakhin – Moscow,
Director of the "Hudlit" publishing house

I am following the creative achievements of Raushan Burkitba-yeva-Nukenova with a huge interest and proud starting from her first collection of poems "The arabesques of love" (1996), "Love - a nomad" (1998), "Night mirrows" (2001). She possesses a unique literature gift that revealed itself not only in her gentle, vibrant and poetry, which is opened to the whole world, but also in prose – both documentary and modern. Her audience is constantly growing because Raushan's poetic creations have already become popular abroad. In 2002, her wonderful book called "The mystery of night" was issued in "Ogoniok" Publishing House of Moscow… The poems, essays, stories and novels of Raushan Burkitbayeva-Nukenova carry the message of "love and truth of pure learning…"

V. V. Badikov – The member of the Writers' Union and Pen-club of Kazakhstan, the Professor of Russian and World literature deparment in the Kazakh National University named after Abai

Raushan,
I am greeting each person, who loves poetry and writes poems. While practicing literature, the person improves him/herself and the world around making it more humane!
May good success attend you!

Olzhas Suleimenov – Almaty, 04.02.2015

The whole watercolor palette of Raushan Burkitbayeva-Nukenova's book of poems encourages us to a certain understanding and perception of our complex reality by means of harsh strokes and sounds – her own preferred picture of world with the predominance of hopes and harmony colors.

Dyusenbek Nakipov

Raushan blends war and peace, cruelty and softness, rudeness and tenderness with the gorgeous talent and internal pain that are appropriate to her. She praises the greatness of Soviet people, their resistance, sincerity, dedication and commitment glowing in her heroes' eyes. Raushan always follows the inspiration of her heart contrary to mind's ash. With certainty of master, she reveals the archeology of buried feelings. Her stirring imagination makes up the lack of knowledge. Achieving the momentum of infinity, she sings about the secret horrors of a human heart in order to guard us from the power of darkness.

Atanas Vanchev de Trasi – Paris

We may experience the tones of feelings from the native affiliation with the history of East that are forever binded with author's own life. Raushan may seem delicate, but her clarity and resielence impresses: "And I will firmly overcome this given term", although "the arrows are flying through the rings of centuries!". In Raushan's new book, you can feel the arm of artist, find a stunning clarity of forms, maturity of compositional principles together with young inspiration!

Valeriy Dudarev – Moscow, Chief Editor of "Yunost'"

The drowsy Asia has woken up; she tries to communicate the things that were like a lasting echo or the echo of faraway olden time, voicelessness and nonbeing. From behind the mountains, which are marked with a purple edge, the sticky sun of East is peeking like a yolk egg. Raushan is a rose, soulful, tender, a little bit extravagant, capricious in her compelling beauty of Eastern woman, who knows that she is beautiful, and what counts most is that she is a poet.

Igor' Mikhaylov – Moscow, Deputy Chief Editor of "Yunost'"

The poet of a new Kazakh era gifted with an exuberant talent shining bright with the songs of heart, warming with the beams of pure soul and curious spirit that rises towards the tops of the world of poetry. I am remaining a fan of your singing and scintillante poetry!

Zhadyra Daribaeva – The author of national anthem of Kazakhstan

> "In the shell of everyday speeches,
> In the epicentrum of vain talks
> Like falcons in the flock of rooks
> These words manifest temperaments."

Tenderly yours, Adol'f Artsishevskiy

Raushan's poetry is very dynamic. She is able to sense reedy motions of soul, gentle breeze, the shining of stars and other celestial bodies that are presented in her poems. They brighten with the originality of comprehension and reflection of the realm, recency of drama and mediativity.

M. I. Uyukbaeva – Professor of Philology at AGU

Raushan lives in the world of feelings and colors. Her soul is gentle, passionate and responsive. She is similar to those trees representing the real notion of femininity, elegancy and grace. Raushan is often inspired by nature, leans towards the blade of grass, gives ear to trees and takes a closer look at the coastal riparian woodlands.

Umit Tazhikenova – The member of the Pen-club of Kazakhstan

A Forward of First Expressions

Spirits like to party! They dance to the music played on drums. They also laugh at the light cast through film. All inspiring some critics to claim oriental spirits sing whenever flutes and fiddles are recorded before a live, appreciative, audience. Partly explaining, perhaps, why these Holy Principalities actively seek to engage with Abstract Expressionism in each of its innumerable forms. Quite unlike the deeply traumatic obsessions of DaDa, Surrealist mind-mapping, or, more recently, transhumanist digital iconography (never to minimise our own beloved Banksy's genuinely auto-empathic graffeti), the highly evocative calligraphics of Expressionism strongly suggest supernatural sensibilities have always gone hand-in-glove with any real search for qualitative states of consciousness. At the risk of slightly misquoting Cardinal Newman (1801-1890) therefore, cultivating such "elative" faculties reveals a road to Paradise. Hence, these divinized monads observably empower radical creativity from behind our manifest sphere - in their own pursuit of things Good, Beautiful and True. In other words, they want to learn, along with us, how to express themselves in a way leading to being "gruntled": a term best defined in our era as a form of self-rapture.

Certainly, in painting and poetry, Abstract Expressionism always seeks to picture our world from challengingly subjective positions. Occasionally even risking distortions of fact in order to achieve a radical heightening of mood, or concept. The overall aim, of course, remaining a portrayal of Meaning, emotional experience, and intrinsic Value; rather than depictions of those incidental mechanisms characterising physical space. In which case, the gifted Kazakh poetess Raushan Burkitbayeva-Nukenova simply needs to take her rightful place among current champions of Expressionism's 21st century revival. After all, her long overdue English language debut will do little apart from enchanting avant-garde readers. Indeed, Raushan Burkitbayeva-Nukenova's book The Wormwood Wind stands against crude positivism and the debased Naturalism so prevalent in contemporary literature, through its flagrant use of sound gradation: allied to a choice of words selected for their sheer melody. All evidenced, by her verse-scenarios, which juxtapose consonants and vowels via playful techniques more reminiscent Matthias Grünewald (1470-1528) and El Greco (1541-1614), than other wordsmiths. Nevertheless, Burkitbayeva-Nukenova's strangely diagrammatic angst has well-grounded historical contexts beneath its linguistic jazz.

Discerned so, this candid collection is clearly the literary outpouring of a planetary citizen. A woman equally at home on the Steppes of Central Asia as much as the Capital cities of Europe. To my mind, a far from trivial verity once we recognise the innate femininity of her versification. Similarly to Sappho (5th Century BC), Burkitbayeva-Nukenova allows everyone access into a woman's world, wherein seductive complexities of thought becomes manifest through wit and rhetoric. Admittedly, her images are often sharp—carefully elaborated for their own jovial sake. Moreover, she has the habit of quoting conversations (imaginary or real) to gain an almost naked immediacy in front of her readers. Yet, in a myriad of manners dissimilar to the Greeks (who apparently prized an unbalanced, one-sided, or exaggerated, mode of perfection), Burkitbayeva-Nukenova stands shoulder to shoulder with Viking peoples when they contend only heroic lives can deal with apparent antinomies. For us, "To Be" is "To Do" and "To Do" is "To struggle" ….. a sense of fated destiny we apparently share with our Kazakh brothers. Either way, Burkitbayeva-Nukenova seems to believe battling for an honest personal "Becoming" is the hardest of all wars to win.

A single unstated assertion runs throughout The Wormwood Wind, arguing, amid its lyrical nooks and crannies, we are only fully human when our imaginations are free. Possibly this is the primary glittering insight behind Raushan Burkitbayeva-Nukenova's collaboration with hidden Restorative Powers above her pen. No one would doubt, for example, when she hints that the moment schoolchildren read about their surrounding environment they are acting in a healthy and developmental manner. Likewise, when she implies any adult who has the courage to think "outside the box" quickly gains a reputation for adaptability in their private affairs – hardly anyone would doubt her. General affirmations demonstrating this sublime and liberating contribution to Global Text will prove dangerous to unwary readers, while its intoxicating rhythms and rhymes will lead a grateful few to elative revolutions inside their own souls. Thus, I unreservedly recommend this ingenious work to Western readers.

David William Parry
London 2015

Raushan Burkitbayeva-Nukenova

The Wormwood Wind

edited by David Parry

London 2015

HERTFORDSHIRE PRESS

Published in United Kingdom
Hertfordshire Press Ltd © 2015

9 Cherry Bank, Chapel Street
Hemel Hempstead, Herts.
HP2 5DE, United Kingdom

e-mail: publisher@hertfordshirepress.com
www.hertfordshirepress.com

The Wormwood Wind
By Raushan Burkitbayeva-Nukenova ©
English

Edited by David Parry
Translated from Russian by Vassiliy Lakhonin
Design by Aleksandra Vlasova
Illustrations by Kristina Glazunova

*British Library Catalogue in Publication Data
A catalogue record for this book is available from the British Library
Library of Congress in Publication Data
A catalogue record for this book has been requested*

ISBN 978-1-910886-12-0

Printed by Mega Printing in Turkey

The Wormwood Wind

Chapter 1

The soul – a wild nomad

***

Every soul – a wild nomad!
Besoting us with repeated tales,
Of nights guarded through a lattice.
Where charms without music or words,
Anticipate abundant marvels
In a a dusty garden smelling of Dzhida.
Where ripening through bitter agony
Grows a purple, red-hot pomegranate.
Oh, you, night beauties,
Like the emerald vine!
Tipsy young men become stupid,
Once enticed by hazel eyes.
But I fly like a bird
Fliting across a sunny river.
To arrive like viscous light
With a pear-colored thread on my arm.

***

And where are you, childhood …
Next door, perhaps?
Water freezes in backwaters.
Where looks grows turbid,
like blinking insomnias –
In fatal ponds of memory.
I remember our revelations
And the fragrance of night gardens.
The assurances of naive love,
A bumpy trip on sleepy trains.
And rattling wheels, the stanitsas
Flashing outside, landscape
Changing, shouts, things, faces.
The moon as a lantern – a speechless guard.
Until night came as a cloud.
And, while raining reverie,
The soul took flight – a sacral case,
Gratuitously gifting existence!

***

The snow was inevitable
Covering doomed fields.
While wood whirled in shamanic dances,
And poplars turned white by candlelight.
How they crackled in their fright,
Those logs thrown in the stove.
As night madly begged the snowstorm
To let the warmth linger.
Oh, unhurried smoke and homeless flakes
Spread my sadness wide.
Let my dying look freeze in windows –
Like the icy veil of a Bohemian fresco.
As snowflakes dance gracefully free:
Yet you are mechanically sad.
Allowing half-lost memories,
To disturbe our gentle quiet.
"And again obsessed traveler"
You hurry for a frantic call,
Still uncomprehending loves ways!
So, snowstorms cry across time …..

Raushan Burkitbayeva-Nukenova

***

The steppe is bounded in steel armor,
Rigorously welcoming winds of change.
Yet, it does not hear word-arrows,
Poisoned, as they are, by everyday betrayals
And intoxicated with fright.
Silent centuries spilled in the vastness -
By bubbling geysers of healthgiving water!
Exhausted not through foolish quarrels,
They still wash stripes and cure our people.
Oh, wise fountains never run dry!
Let the sky keep you in everyones mind!
Each grievance a drop – simply sharpening stone.
The Creator uses everything available, they say:
Spring seeing camelthorns grow in deserts,
While purple-flowered dzhantak* gives honey!
But mystics find truth by being out of sight,
Escaping from temptations, talks, and fights…

*Dzhantak – a camelthorn (in the Kazakh language)

Luggage

Abandoning settled nests,
After smelling the scent of a silver emshan,
Our ruler* left his throune to visit the steppe.
Wearied by melancholy for an abandoned Stan.
Dissolving in fog amid the nights, the roads,
The pathless thickets of biting salt trees.
All hiding internal knowledge: secret lines,
Curiously weakening nerves as if from a chase.
Through sweet rose-coloured smells.
Yet, recovering my breath and fed by summers power,
There, by herdmans fires before daylight
I imbibe the ancient epos: kiui sung on a dombra.
I will run away from urban dust, the swelter,
Where the arrogance of prestige is stacked into storeys.
I will away from every noise. Enlightenment will descend -
The steppe is so calm, raised like a mountain!

Baibars I, Sultan of Egypt (1223-1277)

At the coastal tugai

All day I was rushing to see you,
in sweat and in dust ...
The sparks of a star behind the moon,
stood still, laughing.
And over the cool river -
your voice is clear.
And the branches bend over the water,
like your slim figure.
A soft sound is coming out of your mouth,
a tight braid is behind your back.
And you trust me,
my dear.
The night will untwist its dreams,
just like your braids.
And the stars in thier altitude are turning
into morning dew.
The moon is blessing us with its gentle light,
so we are all enlightened.
And a hot-blooded horse is waiting for me,
by gnawing the bits.
Let the wind carry over
sounds of bracelets to me,
Where a tender song lives
among those herbs of summer.

Tapestry

I didn't mean to be taken prisoner by nomadic hordes -
But was conquered through your handmade tapestry!
By threads from ancient times
Unravelling like dusty that waft into noble banners.
Here clouds of wool pull at hands,
Recoiling under preserved local optimism :
Between anxious thoughts tangled in thorns.
Oh, let the moon measure invisible revolutions.
And a sad song play like a bird
Or fast horses crossing a field.
Where tracks are soaked with bitter tears:
«I believe you will come back by sunrise!»
As arrows fly through centuries.
Our loved ones are waiting at home.
Hidden from the gaze of illicit meetings
Like stars twinkling on a river.

Raushan Burkitbayeva-Nukenova

Tamgaly Tas*

Trying to imagine you, my distant ancestor!
Through messages in your ageless rock drawings.
Of horses racing through centuries,
 while the moon is barely seen.
People are mortal, truly
But ancestral spirits in cosmic sanctuaries dwell eternal!
Maybe I can comprehend the value of sacred totems,
Serving as a covenant: the paradigm of steppe customs.
As I try to find what was valuable for me.
To reconcile my days with my shadow.

What did you want to convey, how did you live?
How can we cognize such unknown depths?
In drawings being destroyed by the wind, snow, rain...
We want to see each other: we share this impulse,
From the moment of birth until old age!
Don't disappear! Speak about rock paintings,
While waiting for our offspring!

Tamgaly tas petroglyphs by the river Ili near Almaty

***

At the coastal tugai
In all my shyness
I will wait for you in silence.
My beloved one, tired of toil and turmoil,
Rush to meet me at the boat of desires

***

Have you seen how apricots blossom in spring?
I was captivated by their beauty yesterday.
And in the morning she untwisted her braids:
now darker than night -
Oh, my friend, your sister has turned into
                                    a beauty!

Date

Stay with me for one more hour.
While the moon is aslant in windows –
Like slowed down slides:
While sand streams tenderly,
Without a whisper of sorrow.
Again, a fairytale night!
Send us draughts of joy,
To prolong our delights.
Then invisible energies will surge through our bodies,
Until we fall asleep utterly exhausted.

***

Let me present you a necklace of magical nights
My beloved one
The light of scented candles is gentle...
Our house, awakened by the sound of keys,
Is always protected by the moon.

***

I look at the moon as in a mirror.
And see your angelic face in it.
Only the cuckoo ruthlessly
Interrupts this moment of pleasure.

***

You are gone but your flavor remains.
Yet after a summer storm, roses smell sweet.
Moonbeams touched my cheek,
As if gently wiping away my tears.

***

There is no sound in the fall garden.
Although a wild goose cried at sunset sky.
Unbearable, this long separation.
Since promising me, my beloved: "I'll be back!"

Presentiment of spring

Like a plucked leaf -
That day we spent apart.
A whistling of contrary winds,
That night in the arms of boredom.
Yet, when dreams arise in sleep
You greet the dawn.
While to rendezvous with spring
All avenues remain open.
Lonely and singing
An orphaned wind outside.
Calls its friend
From the twentieth apartment
To fly together
Over this silent capital.
Hey, no need to suffer
Over newspaper pages!

***

Bushes pout under the windows,
Brushed, as they were, by wind - but so carelessly,
But light rain, short-lived like a dream,
Was covertly caressing, devoted, and gentle.

***

Icy apathy
Invisibly bound the river of love.
An indifferent oval, like a ring
Merged with depthless melancholy.

***

The long-awaited February snow!
A frightened beehive ...
In the underground cafe on the table
Chairs are turned over!
Tunefully rattling
Glasses at the bar.
Now everything is indifferent:
Lies, narcotics.
Snow vanishing at midnight,
Allowing the whole city brightens up by morning.
Through the grief – a forgiving laugh.
A hope for advancement is in the air.

Raushan Burkitbayeva-Nukenova

***

Not the branch, but the string broke …
My hand dropping like a lash.
Shadows sliding like swarthy seals,
I have felt grief.
The wind hysterically blows over a river,
Carrying its pain across the strings...
A yellow leaf stuck to the glass.
Life without you is mostly impossible,
No power can get you out of my mind,
but my heart wants -
To sink like snow into the arms of night.

Hotel

Still full of anxious expectations, hope,
A carousel of songs,
The hotel stores warmth from past meetings
As it waits for its next guests.
Trails through alleyways are not yet marked,
The creaking of wheels floats in cold darkness,
While night robes are thrown onto a chair.
A candle is burning on a celebratory table.
A new century is like a new guest,
Who walks frightened in the dark,
And pokes a frozen finger randomly,
And lives a sleepy destiny
And, at the sound of a new score,
Causes shadows to wander through
ghostly distances.
New calendar days groan like equipment
Turing on the scales of eternal land...

Raushan Burkitbayeva-Nukenova

***

Autumn rain –
A strict maestro,
Arranging the roads
In musical staff,
It chants the melody from a sheet.

***

Oh, why is this bed so cold
And this peg a colored silk cover!
And outside an uncontrollable snowstorm,
All night in anguish, tossing, howling.

Smog

Smoke stratifies in a chilled sky,
While snow is so touchingly clean.
Filling up the capital by morning,-
With a new sheet ready for printing.
Yet growing dark would be a shame
For snowmen - since year after year,
They allow pine trees in parks to green.
Oh, who needs rough copies
When fear and acid rain will disappear.
And blessed paradise will return to us.
Blinding everyone with its carefree smile.
Garden blooms, do not die!

***

Until the flames of our lips are joined,
Until our hands are tied together,
Until the moon keeps her cold silence -
Let this night last until the end of our date.
Let forgotten worries drown in snowy darkness,
Let cars by the roadside park in silence.
A favorite breath will quench the thirst,
As snow in the window flies to its first date!

Raushan Burkitbayeva-Nukenova

***

Everything was so lovely,
Calm and light ...
Yet, falling passionately down from the sky,
Of a sudden, snow covered the city.
As a whirling storm,
Mixing in its snowball,
All plans, reunions of friends,
Even Kaztelecom - which became deaf.
Refusing, however, to demount the road,
To abandon our razzleing,
                    we continued strolling.
Multiplying the jams.
We pined like in prison.
Rebellious slaves
Caught by fate.
We believed that blizzards
Will spin both of us around
And bring out to the edge
Of common paths and words.
Meetings almost predicted for us
In a puzzle of prophetic dreams.
Each clue getting closer,
On the other side of a gloomy glass.
Winking with its tender glance,
Like a chandelier over a table.

06.02.2007 Aktobe
Today we had a guest
Abdizhamil Nurpeisov!

***

Night falls like hopeless melancholy,
While stars march in a permanent patrol.
A soul strays where extreme darkness.
And vapid conversations quieten over the river.
Old moon is filled with fairy light.
Again making its way across silvering waves.
Like a Holy image inspiring a poet,
Yet, he will be able to asleep till morning.

***

A branch knocks at my window
Covered in pink blooms ...
Oh, where is my neighbor
With eyes holding secrets?
The one who was so friendly
And affectionate with me?
But only rain is rustling shyly
Behind those white walls...

***

Oh, how reluctant you are to leave bed,
Like the bumblebee, immersed in nectar!
If only it were possible to stop time...

***

What am I trying to discern
Through these dead recitations - like a blizzard
Of words interrogating a cheat,
Caught at odds by his tricky wife?

***

Shades playing on a bench...
An elder man sleeps in his spring garden,
Wearing a colourful embroidered skullcap
Nestled in the greens.
There are crowds of lovers in lanes-
Some rush to a date,
While echoing these rainbow ideas,
As their day trembles.
I hear insinuating whispers
As well as some sonorous rhymes.
Yet, noise and laughter were not distracting,
As again, sweet Muses demand dominion!

The Wormwood Wind

***

Somewhere cicadas are chirping,
As if delivering roulades.
Yet, bunches of ripe grapes are filled with juice
While stars and leaves fall down
Turning yellow in dust by the fence...
However, human hands
Tear her girlish dress impulsely,
And exhausted by the bliss,
Night opens its arms...

Raushan Burkitbayeva-Nukenova

To Madina

This house is emptiness,
Only ghosts wander passed its black windows.
And the dim moon twisting its mouth
Starts a conversation with you.
About previous tenants who were bored
Among the thickening snows,
Like young rivers warbling,
Being tired of their long-lasting fetters.
Around blazing fires
Disputes refused to fall silent at night.
Flaming glances burning
Then fading in the twilight of yards.
While this house recovered its life in trembling rivers,
Watching a flexible moon in windows.
Like welcome guest ... like flying rain.
That wet wall will hold.

The Wormwood Wind

***

Like a blind rain
In one touch -
You could not quench the thirst of dreams.
Again, I am looking forward to meeting you,
But you fly, fly, fly...

Raushan Burkitbayeva-Nukenova

Ayman Musakhodzha
Gaukhar Murzabek

River of sound

The sky is as taut as a lively canvas,
The sunset bloodred, the lights like ramps.
The clouds floating, the river transitory bliss,
All familiar melodies of the brightest days.
An extravaganza of dance, light, symphonics,
And seagulls seeminly planned like dreams,
A single ensemble on a fairy background.
The sounds, wind, waters are merging.
A magical night of intimate feelings,
Embraces opened like the bending of a bow.
A sorcerous power of love and art,
The river is polishing its pearl like cantatas.

04.07.2008
10 Year Anniversary of Astana.

The Wormwood Wind

***

I will melt into the night air
And become a sensitive silence.
I will leave this boring apartment,
Fading like the unseen string.
But I will miss you,
Annoyingly, like a blow!

Raushan Burkitbayeva-Nukenova

Astro – nomer

All day long among heaped books,
Like roads drawn by manuscripts.
Our tired, blinded mole,
Our scientist, lay down on his couch.
Waiting for star-curtains to be re-opened.
Reviving him with the glitter of remote worlds.
Representation of celestial bodies, faces like Trinity,
So, inserting himself into eternity
                              – remaining silent, rugged,
Watching for answers beyond the Milky dune,
A trace of the invisible always tempted his dreams:
A quick glance breaking through fogs.
And responsive calls flying from heavens heigh.
From Galaxies in our boundless Universe.
From trembling time stealing moments,
Tearing up space, imperishable,
Becoming music: a cheerful rain.
Let the centuries get stuck in unsteady dunes,
He will still hear from the dark wilderness
Containing songs from the stars,
To illuminate his kindly soul!

23.09.2014

The Wormwood Wind

***

To Dariga Nazarbayeva

Your voice can stir the soul,
Can refresh like gentle waves.
Oh, the splash of happiness,
It is so possible,
Like a moment gifted by you!

***

Old moon rainbow -
Like a necklace,
Adorning a blanched face.
Images of the beloved have so many faces!
Will new colours be enough? I feel afraid...

Raushan Burkitbayeva-Nukenova

In a thunder-storm

Birds shrink under rooftops,
While rain stubbornly strikes into rhythmic steps.
A whistle of wind through thunder-blasts,
As hail in grass fills up the trace.
Echos chorusing from steep slopes,
Against contoured mountains darkening -
Far, far, away.
Behind delineated rays of lightning
Which blind and threaten discoveries in the Ili.
Yet, this river and its kurgans guard
Lost secrets from ancient times.
Reminding me even caravans of gloomy clouds
May pass over canvases with victorious banners.
Leaving the countryside calm,
After snow leopards have flashed through our windows.
Yet my apartment lights flared joyfully,
Like responsive warrior-ancestors.

15.07.2008

The Wormwood Wind

***

Turning off the light above my pillow
I wander, like a Jew, in the desert.
Over forty years old, I have wasted even more years,
With the dream of finding my better half!

***

Here, the sun is already glowing with passion.
It went up by the usual route.
But there, all was forgotten - all was dissolved,
I wished night thoughts, but nothing came true...

***

The arrows of our watches rush in a circle.
Oh, so much time has passed ...
A dusty glass is being tarnished.
Gardens keep silence in mystery.
And your soul remains in peace.

Raushan Burkitbayeva-Nukenova

To Marat Bis-engaliev

Shades floating away
In vibratory rivers –
Contours of doubts,
Tremble as arms extend.
We are like strangers,
Our honest glances striking.
Attracted by live music,
Reflected sounds simply pierce.
How valuable the confusion,
This instant is unique.
The rain is granting us forgiveness,
As we stand under one umbrella.
The verticals of mirroring jets
Guarding against strange expressions.
Skies flashing in the dark,
Like your eyes in a moment.
These faerie scenes –
Run like a wheezing bow.
Waves of passion and betrayal,
Make this river a filly.
Galloping off like a centaur
To both dreams and music,
Delightful laurels
And sodden flowers.

06.08.2008

Inter – net

In a captivity of nets and magnetized lines
A boy wanders every night.
By frost bordered gardens falling asleep.
It wants to talk with you,
But does not see, does not hear anyones
Vein requests or futile efforts.
Instead, tacit secrets of the Universal Deeps,
Wherein a myriad lights shine radiant,
Remain ever silent.
But one day, coming down from these screens,
An incredible dream will smile –
And a strange Lady will hurt someones heart.
As an outsider waits on a separate garden bench…

29.10.2008

Raushan Burkitbayeva-Nukenova

***

Will a drop of the dew quench my thirst?
Can you see the moon and the stars in the night sky?

***

It is already night but I cannot fall asleep,
I wander with anguish in my eyes.
And only the Milky Way
Can unite us.

***

Thick shadows roam the asphalt,
The light of faceless lanterns is scattered.
Roads are creaking, overwrought by the alto,
Merging with the sound of awakened doors.

The rain knocks on curtained windows.
And the wind dances in the shadows of branches.
Our garden bench is swollen and wet,
It is not waiting for drunken guests.

The moon disappeared behind mountains.
The poet is asleep, tired of undertakings.
A sleeping city hovers in the clouds.
The latest news is as peaceful as usual.

***

My lonliness is the same as that pine's,
When it bloomed under your window last spring.
Despite bending winds, it keeps stretching.
Oh, it is so persistent,
It is so focused on its dream!

***

At the far shores of the crystal capital
Where there is a new bridge and rainbows shine
The snowstorm will return, Thus, you cannot sleep.
Since roads are already covered with flakes...

***

A rushed day will fade away,
Like a promise.
A kiss will be cold,
A farewell will be reserved.

Raushan Burkitbayeva-Nukenova

To Olzhas Suleimenov

I have been living here for years,
Among words and verbs, burrowing like a mole.
But time flies like a flock of wild birds.
A stubborn man steers his wheels the other way around,
They say,
And women approaches that metaphor in vain,
Calling out his name in frustration, crying in secret.
Only inside books do they find consolation.
Your Muse runs barefoot to the steppe,
They say.
She watches jealously, suddenly sighing, almost with guilt.
Perseverance, patience
– are exemplary for the next generation!
Their voies frightened by an underground rumble.

The microphone was popping; making some pale,
some gray.
Words spoken by regiments from Dunai to the Altai,
Fell silently as they walked through pitchblackness.
According to legend, these phrases have a different meaning,
Disclosing that every secret belongs to men alone!
Again, he expands the concept of space,
He finds roots, the kinship of speech, tribes.
The steppe extends to an ancient kingdom!
So, we are familiar with the consonance of names.

The Wormwood Wind

From A to Z - stretching the universe!
In Our Galaxy - you are the unfading light!
Linking the thread of time, generations,
Furiously working for many years.
He will pack the dawn into his backpack,
To re-illuminate cities from previous eras,
No wonder he is a geologist. He savors the world,
Hoping there is a listener, and that he is not deaf....

Raushan Burkitbayeva-Nukenova

***

Our guest compresses a glass of wine, -
Like comforting breasts.
In the eyes of extinction, there is sadness.
On the couch - like a nail,
She is crying,
She laid down in her longing.
Try to touch her and you will encounter
fire and passion.
In her eyes – there is expression and power!
She would like to drink it all
The luscious juice of those lips.
And the wine grapes - completely
To cut the vine,
That let the teardrop form.
The pollen of her hair
Carried away by a poet.
Of course, he is a well-known expert!
That is not Bordeaux – that is Medoc.
This a fog of Georgian wines.
Premeditating a night of confessions - deception.
Wherein each label is a lie.
Do not disturb memories.
The hallway and walkthroughs became empty,
Steps, to the alley.
The night went out for a meandering walk.
In Lido a cancan is squealing
As the poet fell into a trap!

***

Again there is a wave
                    Of unruly hair -
Autumn woman
                    Is an abundant harvest!
Wine berries
                    Are mature in a vat.
Plucked by a brush
                         Lying on the couch -
A gift of the hot summer,
                    Sung by a poet!
Lush gardens smell
                    Like Antonovka.
Where among grass
                    Tracks are lost.
A gentle dawn
                    With its patterned shadow
Will reward you again
                    With inspiration ...

31.01.2015

***

What a vibrant moon
Blinding everybody with beauty,
Like an apple on the pressed grass!
As silence yawns with anticipation…

***

At the bottom of a transparent glass,
Like the petals of a tea rose,
Forgetting the terrible cold,
Tea leaves are waiting for their singing lessons.

And their secrets are disclosed,
They dance, remembering the summer.
The fever of burning synchronous views.
The smoke of elastic cigarettes.

Shadows game in the bushes of jasmine,
Motivated by forgotten romance.
And the rustle of crumpled muslin
Abandons the afternoon to a state of trance.

And a passionate whisper by the fountain,
The embarrassment of gentle shade
A hue of hidden deception,
Aside the intoxicating smell of lilacs.

These ups and downs,
Like a ritual nocturn.
Allow tealeaves to crave for Sunday.
When everyone wants summertimes return!

Kabardino-Balkariya, Chegem,
July 2003

Raushan Burkitbayeva-Nukenova

At the pasture

Their Yurt is covered with white felt.
A fine-fleece smoke, like a thread flies,
Coiling in a blizzard. A singing string
Dombra notifies relatives about the wedding.
But the snow is piled up! And the paints are lean.
While the village is deeply immersed into a dream.
And the Kremlin-Prague sailed as a mirage.
Esaul has been terrifyed with the storm.
And the steppe is silent, let the winds blow.
Although in their yurt everyone felt stuffy.
The canopy is folded, so that a creaky cold
Would leave people alone in its folds.
Feelings bubbling up like oil in a cauldron.
The pattern of each ornament – an ancient art.
It will encrypt timid words,
So that rumors will bypass you,
Dotted star-lines are marked on the road
As our footprints lead to a frozen threshold.
Our drivers forgotten pager sounds the alarm.
You will not forget this evening!

The Wormwood Wind

Chapter 2

In pursuit of line

***

About everyday prose,
That poetry has entered,
That under my window there is a birch,
Washed by a storm, departed.
Clouded insults have come down with rain
To be grounded again.
Forgetful of what happened before -
I write poetry - I create love!

***

Clinging to your unshaved cheek,
I will forget all my sorrows.
I am grateful for destiny
For that occasion,
For these rainbow sights.
The voracity of our views
And the inevitability of our first meeting!
I yearn to follow my dream,
To squander my tenderness.
To tear clothes, like masks,
To fly over the city tired
And dissolve in your caresses.
To become grass under the snow!

Raushan Burkitbayeva-Nukenova

***

A confused blizzard is swept away.
The machine settled in the snow.
Its wheels are numbered by a dog,
Which I cannot understand.
This dog is from a neighboring apartment
And always carries mud on its feet.
Which makes the owner of the house upset
He lives in a house across the street.
He swears to smear the wheels with chemicals
-that is how he is preparing for winter.

He prepares his car as if he is going to war!
The guard laughing in the darkness.
A war erupts in heat,
Two irreconcilable tenants.
And I am doing PR,
Waiting for a grandson, staring from the porch.

At the bus stop

Mountains of watermelons and cantaloupes
are available at bus stops.
It is evident farmers have not worked in vain,
On their fields.
Nearby! These damsels
Are difficult to pass by.
By thirst, midday heat.
Like fever, we are tormented.
Maidens, lovely maidens...
Stripped to the limit.
And devoured by ones eyes.
Across young men's bodies...

Raushan Burkitbayeva-Nukenova

Almaty

Cars are crawling, the smog is thickening.
My city is sick, it could not bare anymore.
The roads are whitened like bandages,
Under layers of snow bridges are swollen.
Will this solve the problem of isolation?
We are all responsible for a magical conjunction.
There is coldness in heart,
                              coldness in apartments.
Fraud, violence, disputes on TV.
Clubs of fog, the noise of discos.
The whole world is sick: complicated century.
Night games, fun and dancing, are overplayed.
In our own homes, we are like foreigners.
Children move to the West, we move to the East
We move in different directions,
                              looking for the source.
Yet, adamant are the rugged mountains,
We say our prayers in sight of them.
In anger, they only move their shoulders,
And we cannot sleep at night due to fear.
Although, the sun will rise and snow will melt,
While our doubts will be diluted in the river.

The Wormwood Wind

Astana

The steppe, by dropping its snow covers,
Under the gaze of the sun, has blossomed.
Nearby, a capital renewed by
Palaces of marble and glass.
Age old rivers and lakes, awakens,
Although its trails lead us to ancient times.
Where shepherd's songs are sung amid mountains.
Yet, discoveries are ahead.
And villages are full of hope.
New villagers have returned, like fledglings.
While fields are as noisy as they should be.
Newspaper pages are flying around.
Dreams rush upwards.
Records shine with gold.
Let our Ak Orda,
Play the sounds of spring chords!

Raushan Burkitbayeva-Nukenova

In London

Soul trembling like a chick,
After finding itself in a tunnel.
With neither sun nor scope inside,
Making Kazakh flesh and mind riot.
My wet shirt is dirty
My soul laid down after being dropped from clouds.
My son is bored, eager to go home,
Here the world is different; everything is different!
I caught the sadness of the songs
Just like a strain
The sounds of home,
Their images are familiar, their motives.
When we are together, we are happy.
On your birthday, my dear!
Your sadness, and my tears,
Will gave way to the rainy clouds.
Here everyone is pale; the roses have no fragrance,
If they move to Astana,
They would die because from its coldness!
Yet, we shall heat it!
Such a life, where every minute is counted.
For a steppe person – that is the end and a burden
Where each moment is weighted like a object.
Oh, you cold Brits!
Kings and beggars,
And your island – is like a jail to me!
So much arrogance; without blemish,

And of poor Diana?
With her immense kindness.
She was a bright light
She lit the falsity like a miracle,
She merged with azure heights.
But luxury and diamonds do not warm,
Oh, the palaces, churches, and atlantes.
You are so lonely amid the crowd.
Here the world is cold and cruel.
Only powerful ambitions ripen,
Shakespeare and "The Beatles" remain giants!
Although, among the lawns and taxis.
The rushing crowds,
Like rain dropping from the sky,
You are a drop of vital blood in that mix.
Where African couplets
Sound loud like booklets.
Where musical lions reign on stage
Yet, you are afraid of the voracious hyena
Afraid of applause!
While rewarding the stage with compliments.
The theater is full There is power in freedom.
You are a great king among the beasts.
But the truth is near – by the door,
Not under the mercy of nature.
It will let everyone sleep peacefully -
At the hotel, palace, prison, in bed.
In dreams; in my dream you are on a horse,
But in real life – are you often tied down.

Raushan Burkitbayeva-Nukenova

Destiny being short -
Too short for some hopes to come true.
- And why has all this happened to me? -
My heart is full of grievances, separations.
Old age - is a network of wrinkles and suffering.
London tends to make everyone upset,
It groans with forgotten fractures.
Yet, Russian snow makes the spirit stronger,
While longing for a cup of tea to warm itself.
No wonder one-eyed Nilson
Experienced the heat of distant cornfields.
If you are brave enough, however, and not lazy,
Its better to go to India, to the elephants,
Where gems and playful silk abound.
In return, grant us tolerable bills.
Without any need to guess who is better.
No wonder the sons of Jewish and Chukcha people
Bought out English clubs.
Precious stones price all -
With which good Abramovich decorated
The fingers and ears of lovely maidens.
Although, it looks like Russia became too tight
Causing many Russians to move to Britain,
Where oligarchs are loved and respected.
Where vodka "Glasses of Grammovich" are served -
And Berezovsky sends his greetings,
By splattering his saliva into a microphone,
Forgetting the Old Testament,
About radiation and background noise.

Britons moan in pubs,
They completely purged the entire season.
And there is no reason to bet.
Their lawns dry out because of no rain.
Their interest in boxing is lost,
Fidel is to blame: the progressive.
Now, players and every actor,
Receive tepid impartial reviews.
Rendering true judgement impossible.
True judgment, of course, warms our souls.
When disputes and rumors get extinguished,
And bookshelves in bedrooms are emptied,
Other people will come,
                    with their own likes and dislikes.
Contrarily, mind evaluates everything.
All fervor will subside – the soul will get tired.
Flowers, and their fruits, will wither in dust.
Since London sleeos like a sad perfumer,
Actors, players, and a hypocrite.
Madame Tussauds – is so farsighted.
But you will feel sick and sad,
That just like a wax doll,
Dreams are encased for centuries.
And they are so lifeless, terrible.
Boxing, football, even war, is better!
Furious is the reproach,
Of the ancient pyramids' descendant.
And the trading house, Grandfather Al Fayed -
Living for centuries without any trouble.

His sad eyes burning; obscured candles,
From Arabian tales. Although they say time heals.
Does the pain of these infinite processes.
Stir everyone without end?
Like the luster of the British crown.
Outside the window – there is snow, lights,
Where a Russian tsar
Lived out his sad days,
The one who is remembered to history!
And somewhere out there, on Baker Street
Holmes' eyes are full of conjecture.
And a terrible destiny awaits strangers.
Perhaps, an innocent is about to be hung.
Whether by loop, or trail,
Time will eventually tell.
Oh, childhood paradise, a happy delight!
Yet, the howling of the Baskervilles' dog,
Is like a sickly sob from the bottomless swamps.
Human fears – mighty blood-calls.
Oh, where are imperial habits?
Where young lords takes part in a battle of words,
Making rebukes - throwing papers around.
While this iceberg melts like a fiord.
And where does the "Titanic" sleep?
Since no passengers, no stingrays are in the hold.
It became a legend, a mournful past,
Abandoned an antique shop.
Is that because (like a celebration),
I believe in wonderful moments,

The Wormwood Wind

Wherein we all wait for Christmas gifts?
Ah, breath of freedom breathes!
November, rain, preparations,
Oh, may a miracle come, at last!
A patient poet is a priest of revelations
All in all, each tale holds a rainbows end!

24.11.2007
London-Ekaterinburg

Beatles
Solar submarine

In the country of submarines -
                Beneath the waves there is a godsend!
A submarine turning yellow,
                And becoming rusted through tears.
The Beatles told us,
                They went along with it!
Saying mines cringe
                Through skepticisn from the Thames.
A course is set towards peaceful atoms!
                By fleets housed in lost UK strongholds,
Now, in the depths of the sea
                It accompanies the **mermaids**.
A cruise of cloudly currents
                Rining bells for jellyfish.
The submarines are darkened
                And not terrifying anymore,
They are like whales, although the yellow ones
                Remain tellingly absent these days,
Singing in the open.
                With no combat losses!
Guests are greeted by a cruiser.
                It became a star hotel!
To Yoko it would have been a house
                John would have been happy!
Lay down in a cabin on your own ...
                Jacuzzi and sofas -

For extra comfort,
                    like Yoko and Lennon!
But the Beatles' fans remember
                    English fogs,
Lying protests -
                    In a struggle for better worlds.
And even Elvis Presley
                    loved and sang their songs!
Yet, the magic four fell apart,
                    The idol was shot dead...
In our century, when there is no prohibition,
                    you became - a rarity,
The Beatles - on the screen!
                    Romeo and Juliet
Do not inspire the world.
                    Or fans at the cash register,
Police - all wearing helmets.
                    Plastic babies ...
Old man Shakespeare is sad
                    Othello, the king of Lear.

***

The earth is spinning, as nowadays – the discs.
Only dust covers the tracks.
It is a pity that as soon as a talent is discovered – it is at risk.
The grayness of bullets remain native to the devil's horns...

***

A bullet left a point on the pulse.
The rhythms subsided; there is only silence.
Black wheels on the shelves fell asleep.
While idols are escorted away after a farewell song.

***

"All we need - is love!!!"
It became an anthem over the years.
Yet, a sea of fans is roaring again!
They watch us from the hill...

With God's blessing!

When there is pain and slush in the heart,
And the steppe howls like a gray wolf
And the only thing to do is cry.
Instead of you four – only two start to sing.

And aging branches
Will sadly cling to the window.
From the album – like young children,
The Beatles intimates laugh and sing!

His Highness draws a picture
With snow and rain.
We wait for inspiration
From the sky – we wait for an order at night.

He, like you, throughout the universe
Is not accepted by everyone; he is lonely.
His gift – is imperishable spirit,
Saved for general communication.

Let's talk; let the revelations
Rediscover the sound of a guitar.
Our whole life – is one moment!
A song dispelling the moaning wind.

I appreciate, Highness, your participation!
In all daily things.
For the hours of love and happiness,
I need no other riches!

***

A leaden sky above Liverpool.
A leaden acorn ruined your life.
Fired at us, its bullet is aimed.
A constellation chain ripped by a gun!

And they sang blithely!
Like the titles of a film - a life suddenly flashing.
Allowing death to put a lasso on his head.
A heroic detective – discovers hidden sharks.

Industrial city; an evening twilight.
The boys dare – a guitar chord.
With zeal until the early morning.
The Beatles conquer our world; set the record!
To record!

***

The crowd, crushed by guitars,
The magic Four from Liverpool,
Will turn up the heat - so no one can asleep.
And then - couples in pairs
Into history – through a wedding march.
The fans – in a liverwurst march...

Raushan Burkitbayeva-Nukenova

***

Pictured in a black turtleneck -
Open, available near the lantern.
Four knights from English fairy tales.
The sun blinds; our struggles seem vain!

***

Disheveled bullies -
The reward of a British Empire!
Feelings expressed in two ways,
What clothing suits such a reception?
They will not have a haircut!
"Perhaps, we should put on pajamas?

Let's not blow our noses loudly,
And quietly sail with the submarine set...
Or put on a hat,
And appear in front of the Queen!
She will teach us tangential things,
Revealing the rules of etiquette.
She will sing a song in the opening act,
Or will join us singing in the chorus ... "

***

In constellations that are embossed like targets!
During misplaced times – a sniper amongst Rocks!
The villain,
The legend of rock and roll aims at generations -
Getting into the hearts of his family, friends ...

***

The rain is crying alone ...
You were happy with Yoko!
West + Eastern fire!
Who learned the best lesson?
Your flower got wet in the park ...

***

Beatles — are the idols of millions!
Wild screeching - over the stadium,
For all the girls - ammonia,
They could be so annoying!
Pants-pipes, onto the pin -
Microphone, the guitars are moaning.
And with the unkempt mop -
By the underground - to the balcony!
All their fans sing along to their songs,
Repeating these melodies to the same beat!
Linda is singing a lullaby for her daughter,
At home.

But McCartney is celebrating his hit
Among the flocks of seagulls
He is drinking beer in a pub at night.
The fact that her father is famous,
Stella would never understand.
She sews clothes! Wall Street
Will plummet their income.
And in rags of gray boredom
The dog is still waiting for his owner.
Paul takes a guitar into his hands
And quietly sings to his daughter.

***

Were you dreaming of fame?
By flying as the may beetles!
The rain of stars – at a misty distance,
Grouping chords at night.
Liverpool – is the capital of rock!
Four Men glorify,
All this - taking place until one day,
The spiral straightes its line!

***

The sun ripens as a purple cherry
A fever puffing in desert sands.
Escaping to a paradise – with an extra ticket,
Where you can find crimson jackets?
And the crowd, stunned by the sound,
Tasting rock 'n' roll as a forbidden fruit -
Beats in the ears by an elastic rhythm.
The stadium is roaring like a pride!
Let us not get mad from the languor,
Our brains affected by the chords until it hurts.
And flowers are thrown from the balconies
Youth from half of the Earth!

Raushan Burkitbayeva-Nukenova

***

"Say no to war!" - said Paul and John.
In couplets of songs -
Against the doublet
A soldiers' token.
Black news from Vietnam
Like blades cutting the hands of their mothers.

***

Someone walked into the wilderness -
>To see through a third eye.

Someone went there
>To fight in a gas mask.

The Jews are fighting by bows -
>At the Wailing Wall.

Why did they nail

>The Christ?

And that one balks.

>Hey! Who's next on the list?

What other sacrifices

>Does an executioner need?

In the name of love

>Babies are crying,

Choking

>In tears and blood?

Se la vie…

To Robert Burns

"In the fields, under the snow and rain,
My dear friend,
my poor friend ..."
"My soul has no rest
All day I wait for someone ..."
"Once again a poet will come to me ..."

Robert Burns

The hours run, the years run...
    To where,
    To where?
Entailing me after themselves,
    But they thaw – such a pity,
    But they thaw – such a pity.
I am ready to fly after my fate,
    My star,
    My star…
I would like to fill the world with you,
    By storing a dream,
    By storing a dream.
I can destroy all the hedges.
    Believe in me,
    Believe in me.
Tests are on the way
    And the pain of loss,

And the pain of loss.
I believe in life and prophetic dreams,
        I sing,
    What I like to sing about!
Rewards are given to us by God -
        Your love
        My love!

***

Calm down,
Cool your ardor.
You lived only,
When you loved!
All the rest of the time -
You were just looking for pleasure.
To whom the nightingale sings in the garden
The roulades,
And the flower exudes its fragrance?
Have you thought about that,
My precious brother?
You cannot turn back the clocks.
Time is merciless like a wasp of a sting.

***

I will not forget the happy moment,
When a fragrant and flowering plum
Filled my stuffy office!
You have been gone, unfortunately, long time ago,
Only your perfume remained...

***

Short is the flowering of cherry!
But you, my beloved one, are so lonely.
The wind blew away clouds of petals,
My beloved cannot hold them back ...

***

With God's grace - a poet!
Glorifies the world.
It snowed on the night of baptism.
To live in love – is your decision.
The howling of bagpipes is felt in ones chest.
A steppe goose will continue its path.
From that Scottish cell – into the felt
There are clouds, heavy; and long is the route.
The wedge, as if a blade -
Is familiar with this path.
A flock migrates every year.
The verse – echoes the verse.
And the poet sleeps not at night.
He is waiting for a signal from the planets.
A tuning fork of his soul.
Death and the tornado would not destroy!

19.01.2015

Raushan Burkitbayeva-Nukenova

***

The river string rings like a flexible moon
In the quiet night.
Unable to withstand passions glow,
A tired star fell down from the sky,
And turned into a pearl!

To Robert Frost

"He is focused on the future. He's a seeker
He is looking for someone alike,
For the one who is looking for someone else
And finds the one who is alike.
His whole life – is about the search for searches. "

Robert Frost

I decided to watch the sunrise one morning.
      Although dawn barely touched the black pine trees.
Cattle were driven by women from the yard!
School kids were rushing to school,
      Yet, everyone wanted to escape to the river.
The shepherd walks softly singing a song,
      Urging his sleepy farm into life.
That is the plot – the bulls.
His blood still contains some cognac.
      So, I followed him without conceit.
And the sun inflamed the brain of a poet.
      But sleepiness is about to knock him down, and
the shadows beckon him.
The warmth is absorbed by his fruit in summer.
The earth is heated by the energies of heaven.
So, the poet had fallen asleep, thus wasting another day.
So, a miserable shack sleeps the whole day
      Covered by cracked tar.

The shack does not care whether it is the heat, the rain, the storm, or the blizzard...
The resin keeps track of his friend.
It looks into the distance for nature...

Nostalgia

Nostalgia, nostalgia …
In the places that do not exist.
Black braids are tight.
And wonder lights my eyes.
I will make my way through the streets
In between old houses.In my ears there is an echo
The creak of truck wheels.
These people are dear
Although, here I would unable to meet them.
Yes, and we are very different.
So, who will greet us?
Perhaps behind the turn
Mothers voice will call us out ?
The woman who rushes home after work,
To appear for a moment.
She will make us fried bread, muffins
A whole lot more.
She will hand us jam to taste
And distract us from sadness.
From sunrise to sunset
Surrounded by dear people.
How painful are the losses.
Nostalgia, nostalgia...

Raushan Burkitbayeva-Nukenova

There is no easy road...

It is raining outside the window,
Raining falling from heaven.
What happened to you my friends?
Or have you contacted the devil?
From the high peaks in the sky
You have been pushed down.
There must be a reason,
Or a conspiracy, a caprice.
But, there is no road back,
My rains, snow,
Were from native shores
Strictly for us.
What are you looking for, the lost ones,
For the Garden of Eden or a Paradise?
Where is the true happiness,
Yet, they demolished our house, barn.
They stacked woodpiles
Floor after floor.
At night we slept poorly,
We are afraid of a knock to the door, of theft.
Drop by drop, like ink,

They will crash us until the end.
Rumors have blackened everything.
There is snow, rains...

27.12.2007

Chapter 3

The herd of prancing poems

***

Let in the herd of prancing poems through empty windows,
Like a fleet of clouds, -
Fake peace is roiled.
And thise burned-out by doubts,
Lacking the studious patience of stone –
Repeat forgotten lessons.
Their lines will flow like rain,.

***

We came out of a relationship,
And birds flew up in the sky.
Such a brief joy.
And again the grey clouds
Over our new capital,
Swimming as in a river,
Swam ever father!

Raushan Burkitbayeva-Nukenova

Chinghiz Aitmatov

Rivers and lakes are growing small,
Where are the flocks of birds; not locusts?
You loved our steppes, mountains
And juniper thickets of being.
The man of wisdom (creator with conscience) has gone.
The captivating stream has gone silent.
"And the Novel has lasted for more than a century",
Its origin is somewhere in the sky.
You fascinated the world by words, and believed
In intentional purposes for our days!
Measuring the century by high standard,
Without undertones or shadows.
And now standing at the edge of the sea,
You say Good Bye!
Our "White Ship".
And the mountains shake with grief,
Neighboring people have become orphans.

Imangali Tasmagambetov introduced me to Chinghiz Torekulovich during the International Research and Practical Conference on Old Turkic Ancient Manuscripts held in Astana in 2001 at the L.N. Gumilyov Eurasian National University. I read out my poem dedicated to him [Chinghiz Aitmatov]. When Chinghiz Torekulovich knew that I write in prose, he recommended me to combine these two genres in my work. "I write novels, but I cannot write poems", the greates writer admitted and gave me his fatherlike blessing. One additional thing that unites us is my novel "The station of my childhood" – about Lugovoi station [Zhambyl region of Kazakhstan] valuable for both of us, where Chinghiz Torekulovich studied at the technical college far back in the past. A huge charisma and benevolence like warm rays were brimming from his legendary presence. As Chinghiz Aitmatov was used to say, "A person never dies when his/her admirers are living and remembering him/her!"

Raushan Burkitbayeva-Nukenova

To A. Nurpeisov

Furious, roiling Aral!
The killing sun is above you.
You were doomed by an insidious destiny,
And died with the times day by day.
Only one stroke of a predatory pen
crossed out the whole world - mercilessly.
An inexhaustible toiler of goods
Is trying to bring you back
To these cherished and favored shores,
To fill a fishnet with frolicing prey.
Half a century you syllable
The novel-rush of grandeur through
"blood and sweat"!
The cries of gulls that whiten mournfully
Over a pile of rusty and obsolete ships
An alarm bell sounds in those words-accords,
Bitter as salt across ruined fields.
Tirelessly, you darn a fishnet
And send the truth through vocabulary.
- Adults and children are so foolish.
Save them Allah from future troubles!
Rebellious and adamant elder,
"The Old Man and the Sea" - in holistic pauperis.
Abdizhamil-aga - You are our Aral -
A keeper of language, customs and merits!

14.04.2010

In the cafe

Having tired of the frosts iron grip,
The snowstorm tore angrily frozen asphalt.
Fleeing from endless worries and boring prose
Its verbal brakes squeaking as if shouting at asphalt.
Skeletal trees are standing along the roads.
The river looks like concrete blocks.
Go to the cafe and throw the bans.
Warm up your soul,
Throw away troublesome thoughts for a little.
In such a whirl where a voice isn't heard,
A head is floating through this crystal sphere.
Rely on your own heart
Believe a song, vivid smiles, and simple words.
A violin is crying and groaning,
Amber ice is moving on the glass.
By morning the pain will have been remitted
Everything will be different,
And a new waiter will polish those glasses.

26.12.2007

Astana

Raushan Burkitbayeva-Nukenova

March

Evil, cold and biting wind
Sends everybody away from the intersection.
Having putting up collars,
The elderly are groaning towards homes.
Old diseases make them suffer -
Their souls are in hibernation.
Waiting for spring warmth,
Exactly the same as a chilled willow.

***

Let clear light shine in your eyes
As a brilliant and pure thought!
It's an visible feature of conscience
To be happy or unhappy.

***

Even though your head has already turned gray
And steady rains pour,
Autumn will enter very quitly into your life.
But do not wait for the first chill,
As an Indian summer will again waltz us round,
And gossamer threads will touch our temples,
Our dreams will be warmed with love,
And gentle hands will be full of passion.
That golden moment is on emerald leaves
Absorbed with the bright rays of the sun,
A gaze is so tranquil in spite of any difficulties,
And there is understanding in your voice.
And the wind tears mercilessly
My last, bright, and lace dress.
A wedge of cranes flying over me
Interrupts my song with a farewell call.
The roads will be dusted by first snows,
Your traces will disappear in darkness.
As our past warms us,
And black ponds become icy.

Raushan Burkitbayeva-Nukenova

***

Wind tears off September leaves
Like pages of a calendar.
Autumn generously covers the table.
A shy birch has such a graceful trunk!
Waves polish the amber stones.
September evenings burn quietly.
Memory will grind the faces of bright days.
And your footprints will melt on the sand.

***

Smell of mown summer
And the fruits of a spicy autumn
Bars of light fill the sticky combs with -
The traces of honey months.

***

Beauty-moon fades in the sky
It is so languid and modest when
it hides in the clouds!
Wherever a rapid course carries you,
Practice patience before the stars.

***

Your light is reflected in my soul.
The stream, giving revelation,
sings its song in the steppe.
Believe me, I am not afraid of winter coming.
When fields turn white and darkness recedes.

***

Chestnut suddenly dropped all its leaves,
Hid its roots and flowers from snow.
Why is it so painful and hard for us
To leave our posts?

***

The snow will be dancing for a long time,
Displacing fear,
Involving the capital in our dreams,
And burning doubts in the fire.

***

This gentle river
Reflects the clouds,
Retouching slightly
Their fancy drawings.

Raushan Burkitbayeva-Nukenova

***

Let the dye fall
On this impudent streak of grey hair
Mocked by thick henna,
Lets ferret out the secrets of sleepy pines!
Where do dreams fly to?
Maybe they are taken by birds
Into the turquoise of heaven.
Where they melt away without a trace.
Although asked to stay
Through defiant years – which continue
and continue ...

***

White fog has covered high mountains.
And the lovely sleeping city.
Draughts are stubbornly shaking the curtains
In our drowsy flat beneath a snowy roof.
Just the same forbidden and crazy feelings
Hide behind cold and misty eyes.
The light of stars and silent planets will
Always answer a tender heart.
And snow will madly caress our faces.
Oh, if we might become snow at that moment
And fill this gray, gloomy and eternal world
With love and the joy of meetings!

***

A roofer is sitting and smoking on the roof.
He is looking down at the city.
A stately bird is flying to him.
No doubt, magpies know everything about everyone.
Praise be to Allah, they are not concerned about us.
As white wheat has ripened in the fields...

***

Stars shine on shoulder straps,
Stars shine in the sky.
Shooting soldiers at the test site is
Like a challenge to the fragile silence.

***

The tiled stove is cold outside,
Though fire burns and rages inside it.
And you're in the crowd, like a cold lunar surface.
Although tears like water soften your stony soul.

***

Bitter suffering is hidden
Behind a well-groomed face.
Cautious encounters are hidden
Behind diamond rings.

***

Uneven lines - the lessons of weary memory-
Fell across my notebook.
Although, there are no offenses, no illusions,
Only moonlight is fickle.
A lover of pompous phrases is quickly forgotten,
Because there is no faith in wet eyes...

***

What a giant sun,
It warms the whole world!
Sometimes one line
May glorify a modest poet.
And the land is pleased to accept everyone,
Although it suffers various ills.
And the Word sometimes decides -
If there will be a new dawn...

***

Everyone is so lonely in this world!
Twins alone only lucky.
Yet,, God loves everyone,
We need to look for Him!

***

The dialogue we are having
With ourselves is endless.
Thoughts are beating against the ceiling.
And there is silence between two stars...

Raushan Burkitbayeva-Nukenova

***

How can we create comfort in our place?
Where there is love, there is warmth.
In this motley world
The main thing is not to lose ones head.

***

When I look at the cherry leaves -
I do not feel sad or sorrowful.
Only a stubborn star
Repeats my age against spent years.
Night is purring outside the window
And my daughter is hastening to her beloved!

The Wormwood Wind

***

The embankment has been divoid of people for several days.
As ferocious winds summon up fears.
Curiously, there is a smell of sauerkraut in the house.
While breezes hang on the defoliated bushes.
Autumn is finishing and the parks are empty.
And a troubled herd of clouds
Takes the remnants of faith to the steppe.
Draughts alone will fill the void.
Our city has shrunk due to piercing cold.
And the sun pours warmth sparingly on our porch.
Oh, let that stolen kiss
Illuminate a dismal face.

Quasi-fashion

Branches - needles. Voiced motives.
A bright cloak of elegant September.
Thinly clad and beautiful girls.
An aria sounded by a deaf ringer.
Who has been caught in the gossamers,
Flying across dusty pavements ?
Rain deceived by golden leaves
Draws colorful pictures again.
Once again autumn plays its tricks,
Catching hapless guests.
At night a gypsy cooks her magic potions
For harmful and amorous plans.
And stars are flying around sloping roofs.
And mermaids are singing in the river !
Flocks of birds leave their comfortable nests.
As a cold pond is in blossom.

***

An orchestra is playing once again
A suite of night lights!
Stars are gathering crowds.
Flowers are at the doors of the hall.

***

Fate has brought us together,
As two disparate wings,
But fragile bridges have again been ruthlessly
Broken by you
Covering expectations
Through the thick glass of a river.

***

The fall let its
Goldern braids down.
The grass soaked up
Sun and warmth,
The wind threw seeds
Into a river,
The web caught
Old windbreaks.
The rain cut
A bushy armful
Of colorful leaves,
Having spread them around,
Like a packet of
Old and unanswered letters.

And the fires that are behind the river
Completed the circle.

Raushan Burkitbayeva-Nukenova

***

A stream becomes a river,
When it absorbs water.
And we become wiser,
Through the years that give us wisdom.

***

I let you go, let go,
Put you upon the shelf.
I will shut a door silently behind you.
Suppose you will be sought in a shop of losses.

Embankment of hopes

Tonight, the river blinks
With a heavy, glowing, silence.
As motivations found in sad songs
Are dying away in the vasty deep.
The moon is paddling delicately.
A chilled star is trembling.
A tired wave is feeling chatty.
Wires are clinking through sorrow.
And I walk along gloomy embankments.
Gazing at boring lights,
And seeing a good plot
Within windows and doors.
Until sombody's careless glimpse
Will snap me into new hope,
At a forbidden roadside sign.
Staying among the dormant and dusty grasses.
A slender berth will come alive tonight
To rhythmic spanking.
And the lights of this magnificent river
Are predicting a rendezvous again.

Raushan Burkitbayeva-Nukenova

***

Disco music is sounding in the park behind the river,
Like the hysteria of an energetic century.
Rhythms and drawn impermanence
Are shaking the night.
Bodies are trancedly twisting,
Moving in the vortex of tight - breakdancing.
Nowadays behavious stuns old parks,
Rains will wash away this bright make up.
While parks are groaning thereabouts - they cannot sleep
now -
It goes with the new capital.
Street cleaners will sweep leaves in the morning.
Dreams will fly away after hiding in the grass.

***

Oh, why don't I see you in my dreams anymore?
And why do you rarely visit me during daylight hours?
My life is empty, like white pages.
Is there no place for me in it?

***

Saddle a horse
And ride full speed to meet me!
I will return my love to you,
Love me,
Love me...

Raushan Burkitbayeva-Nukenova

Nocturne

Ringing pins are weaving a web
Evening sparkles fresh.
Restless birds are flying in the sky,
Stacks are on the field boundaries.
Shivering branches close tight with sorrow.
Nights have suddenly become longer.
Autumn is playing Nocturne on his piano -
Spreading muted shadows.

***

Fall has come so quickly...
However, our fires burned as recently as yesterday.
Today the sun is closed by a cloud,
Causing a sulky day.
The hours are dragging slowly,
And asphalt looks like coffee grouts.
A gray-winged dove of hope
Flew up through the blackened horizon.
The night has overturned all doubts
Having brought starlit snow.
Chilled shades are sliding away,
And a dull garden is covered with leaves.

28.10.2008

***

Streets pressed by rollers
Are full of vehicles - lighting chained,
Driving slowly.
The rain is dancing, bubbling, and
Jumping from a roof to a step.
In this iron bond
An angry Jeep is squeezed into a ring.
Rain, everywhere, finding its way,
Across grass straining towards light.
And traffic policemen are rigorous today,
Teasing your driving license.
Encouraging moans.
We wll howl down thundering heaven.
While a pedestrian hastens away
From weathered wagons to his home.

Raushan Burkitbayeva-Nukenova

***

I hasten to you through my dreams.
I am free and people do not see me!
The winter is finishing, and stormy spring will come.
Sweep the world! And who will condemn it?

***

Being soaked by the rain and bitter tears,
Our tired city dissolved amongst dreams again.
Waves are caressing our marina of reveries
Where joyful meetings will happen again.

Hunting season

October has come and it is gloomy outside.
Old penny-moon is paling in the sky.
And it is hard to sleep when her sphere is full.
A flock of geese circles over the capital.
You can hear a cry from its leader when half-asleep.
The river is awash with fallen leaves.
While guns shine in distant trenches.
And shots thunder chorally over the steppe.
Hundreds of geese are falling down like droplets,
Resulted in the wild delight of hosts and guests.
Holding their holiday stomachs against reasons aplenty.
There comes a time when a gambling man's hunting season.
Either of them have the same instincts.
Sound as salty jokes in tight quivers...

***

The stars are completely dying away
under the dome of the sky.
Fuss carries us away from the shore of dreams.
A farewell cry of geese will not be heard
any more in their nests,
Where a seagull napped near the gloomy bush.

Raushan Burkitbayeva-Nukenova

***

Oh, waves of tenderness and sails of our hopes
 Please carry us in our boat.
To where we can hear the chattering of birds.
The meadows are in blossom and their scent is so subtle.
Joy and embarrassment do not leave our faces.

***

A road is in our hazy view.
And sleepers are running up a ladder...
And fall is on our doorstep,
And used trains have sadly lined.
And I remember that in the early spring
When our mother saw us off,
We dashed like a green arrow
Into our dreams to catch happiness.
Yet, lips and shoulders have become weather-beaten,
And ghostly vapours have disappeared.
Now, we value rare meetings,
And will give our enthusiasm to youth.
Where does summer go?
It goes to the old train station.
Where our heart is warmed with childhood,
My train is often late for this destination...
However, our lives do not give us rest,
We look for crazy ways, seeking a new line.
I'm sorry, Mom, I'm sorry!
Once again, its time for me to hit the road.
And along the right-of-way
I will see your alert with ever strict eyes,
My guardian angel in a scarf...

11.11.2008

Chapter 4

Generous bazar gift

The Wormwood Wind

***

*"One goes to the bazar or walks up the Kok-Tobe
and the other goes back from bazar or walks down
the Kok-Tobe"…*

Pomegranates, raisins, halva and figs
Are generous gifts from the bazaar!
Under the sun of a copper samovar
We will have a sumptuous feast!
Like tea leaves at the bottom of a teabowl,
Just beckon me with your eyes.
Do not vanquish my hopes
With your eyes that are sweeter than the violet!
And that whimsical moon
Rinsing with wreaths of flowers
Stands against the silver river.
Spring is flying to the foot of the Kok-Tobe Mountain!
It is so hot in the yurt!
The thoughtful wreath is floating down the river
As a life-ring from our encounter.
Do not extend this separation period!
From the shelves of the southern bazaar
An old man is giving
Persimmon, sherbet, Indian tea and
A pair of galoshes for his grandchildren
Instead of those with holes!

Raushan Burkitbayeva-Nukenova

To Tleubay ata, Tyndym apa, Serik

A moonbeam scuttled like an alert lizard
Under the white canopy of our yurt,
Getting out the korzhin
Where the saksaul is sleeping near the hearth
(and squeeking like a mouse in the corner),
We saw a beam sneak to the table like a cat,
Where the kurt and ayran are shining in the dark.
Our chapan is decorated for winter with a fox fur.
Our dombra with its side uplifted is trembling
Along with the felt clouds over the fire.
And the echo sleeps at the bottom of our well
Ready to scare wild wolves
And rescue our flock from death.
Grandfather has set a trap in the ravine
And made a snaffle bit for his grandson.
A tired donkey-friend is snoring.
I will place it in a harness in the morning.
Oue faithful dog awaits for me by the haystack.
Chips are put together like a tower.
Let's go to the mountain - and further on to the forest.
Feeling a fluff of sadness against mature reeds,
A little bird is on the horse croup.
A herd is blackening far away.
The sun has a little run left.
A sleepy river is muttering.
Separation from childhood is faraway

Juniper

Once on a clear spring day
A boy planted a juniper by the window.
He had a long way to go.
The juniper whispered: "Be happy and go!"
And week after week, the years flewby.
Having shed their leaves,
the branches adopted a tranquil melancholy.
The tree, however,
was stubbornly waiting for those familiar steps
Shivering from cold frosty shackles.
And the awe of youthful sticky leaves.
Welcoming everyone with tenderness: "Is this you?"
Perhaps, being tired from the long absence,
Only strong hands can embrace its flexible trunk.
He will rest in the shade on a scorching day.
The juniper was waiting for its sweetheart like a bride.
And finally, with his gloomy eyes bent on the ground,
A man came with an ax in his hands....

Raushan Burkitbayeva-Nukenova

***

A shy and willowy Moon
Reflected in the sleeping river.
And a revived Registan
Changed from day to day.
Its domes and blue panels
Blending into an azure sky.
In the same way as ash
Cleans silver earrings
And makes them sparkle again.
So, with the ash and mould of time.
Minarets go sky-high!
Washed by prayerful voices
through lines of banners,
Forgetting the calls and taboos.
And surahs of our ancient Quran
Shining with brilliant quotes.
Like silk that came from a caravan,
Guarded by your grandfather – a soldier.
Oh, how fragile is this life,
and how careless our world.
Oh, how many people have been killed!
Only the Word will never die.
As a moon disk – a window into ages.

***

Apples are floating down a ditch!
They are bobbing like floats into childhood,

Bitten by shoals of tiny fishes.
Sunblessed kisses are seen on their sides.
I do not mind our garden neighborhood.
Where toads sing their roundelays at night.
Fireflies are in the willows,
Taking the form of cascades.
An owl is hooting,
So, mice are quaking with fright.
A new moon is hanging from the roof
Like a crafted earring.
The heat absorbs
All sweetness in this summer -
A paradise earth is,
My Planet!

***

You still remember it -
This appetizing blood-red marvel.
Oh, what a fragrant Oporto apple
And sweet its life-giving juice!

Raushan Burkitbayeva-Nukenova

***

The autumn sun is not so tiring,
And branches are bent under the weight of fruit.
It's time to gather fragrant Oporto apples
from our gardens.
Before the first night frosts.

***

Captured spirit strays amid building yards,
Their boarded up spaces in street grids.
All displacing poets from their warm beds,
While swarms of thoughts are sweeping old litter.
On the steppes, mountains and scorched desert,
Dances, jumps and roars in wild, free, winds.
Taking the smoky wormwood smell
Floating enthusiastically to everlasting heavens.
Oh, tell me where are the tents, encampments and
Fires along the ways of overweight caravans?
Dead trees are merely sloughing!
Rock paintings are on the Ili River.
Our ancestral territory forever granted!
Oh, how can we preserve these fragile moments
in our world?
Fill rivers with life and moisture
And not interrupt the trembling thread of the fates!

***

My poems sound like responsive echos,
Rebounding on me from the river.
From mountain peaks,
where the shadow of a nut-tree -
Longs for the inescapable...

***

I will raise bridges
By myself.
And will be speechless
Behind my line.

Raushan Burkitbayeva-Nukenova

***

The strong smell of fine herbs,
And heated tandoor, roaring.
Arabesque colours have become pale
A gown has been burnt into black holes.
Turbans were wound as figures
On the axis of roads and dreams.
Also, sour dough is fermenting in vats,
Causing cartloads of flatbread to be ready by morning.
Only Samarkand knows this secret,
And there is no tastier flatbread anywhere!
Emir of Bukhara and Kokand
Looked its secret in flour and water,
But didn't find the paradigm.
- Can your baker tell me the recipe?
Yet, he waited for advice from wiser heads.
And promised a reward for hidden rules.
Perhaps, the answer was the air
Of these places.
A master, somewhere, was laughing.
- Let them solve a puzzle or take a test.
Again, the moon is flying upwards
Above the teahouse like a flatbread.
A baker is kneading dough with a spoon
And painting his mustache with basma, henna,
Questions are showered like stars,
Although, the sky is full of black holes.
And birds are getting off to sleep in their nests,
While only tandoor is still burning at night...

Domes of Samarkand

The pearl trunk of a plane tree
Spotted shadows on the grass.
A pair of inclined minaret domes
Is sailing across the sky.
An Arabic ligature rushes up like a flower
Through eternal prayers.
After the long absence and battles
The Hot East is resting.
Unfortunately, life is not immortal under the moon,
And an architect pugs clay by his hands
To keep his name down the years
And to help us to know.
And what's the use of gold and bullions,
If the well has dried up lacking water?
Tiles came through the fire,
Shining for us like a hymn to beauty.
A visitor freezes!
Going blind becasuse of the sunrise and a sunset,
It is clearly that, the architect was in love!
Thus, his tiles are flawless and radiant.
Turquoise arches and vaults
Hold a heavenly dome to our gaze.
Regenerated water sings
And fine traceries shine with gold.

Raushan Burkitbayeva-Nukenova

***

A cruel tiger tears a deer to pieces,
And there is an arena for fighters.
Perhaps, a tiltyard is intended for battle?
Well, a ball, a field, and a stick is for golf.
Like night and day
One is subordinated into the other as
In Ohm's law.
The order of numbers, words, and characters
For all people is the same.
And behind a high wall
Having enveloped in a single idea,
The harem lives in hope
According to its ancient practice:
Being worthy and equal to the Shah.
During this night - all praises be to Allah!
Giving him one more son,
Trying to ascend into paradise like a bird.
Where a thousand beautiful girls rejoice,
Whose days are colorless and vain.
Their beauty unnoticed,
Oh, they are insidious and dangerous!
Jewelry ever shines.
Although, eunuchs remain formidable deterrents.
Perhaps their hate made these girls pale?
They are jealous to all the poor.
Who work on cotton plantations
Knowing bracelets are the Shah's shackles.

Only Zuleiha is beloved by her husband.
She lives in comfort and does not need a guard.
Amid a host of curly kids,
Her shawl is burnt and has holes.
But, how her eyes glow!
Like ripe grapes.
And every night she is
Utterly in love.
And in the morning she will bake a flatbread.
And sing like a river flowing ...

In the teahouse

The moon teased me with
A fragrant smell of tandoor flatbread.
Like a cheese crust,
Luring a poet into a trap.
Under the shady plane tree
On a pile of colorful blankets
She sat by a trestle-bed
Listening to the sound of dutar.
Getting drunk and swimming in bliss.
Her eyes were blacker than olives,
Her voice was as clear as a stream.
Although, sweat poured off her back,
Accompanying smoke from clay ovens.
You're suggestive persimmon ripens!
Your lips are ripening pomegranates.
Listen, teahouse keeper!
Where is the pilaf and khashlama?
How hot this soulful look!
An apricot is melting on my lips,
And a soft peach is splashing me with juice.
Fluidly, five me a tea of bowl.
Your rings are shining.
Yet, silk hides your body.
At tempting distances.
My soul is singing like a pastoral.
A black veil is trembling.

The Wormwood Wind

***

A voice is heard over Samarkand at night-
Calling to prayer is so exalted.
It chases away dreams and the darkness of nightmares
I am thankful for this.
Five times I bent my knees, my back.
Since I believe, my God, will never leave me.
The only thing I'm afraid of, my friend,
Is losing your love, my queen.
You live in palace, and I – in a desert.
Where evening shelters freeze due to cold weather.
But you'll come back for me with the embarrassed moon,
To start a fire in my soul at dusk.
I time made hot by two loving hearts,
And I will fall asleep exhausted in your arms.
In the morning, a minarets call will awaken me.
We'll never forget this date.
A star will flush and fly under our roof,
As her dress ruffles through the prayers.

04.12.2007

Sary-Agash

Raushan Burkitbayeva-Nukenova

* * *

The captivating maidens of Samarkand,
And charming aromatic tea
Are weaving a carpet, as if they keep secrets,
Accidentally throwing their eyes on you.
Their eyes are impartial and finely-honed
Their movements are full of virtues.
But romantic encounters are predicted for us
Under the growth of a young, pale, moon.
Let your black braids down,
In nude compliment to your pearl body.
Yet, even the beauty of your lovely maidens
Cannot eclipse El-Registan.

* * *

Houses look at each other
In the Uzbek mahalla.
Along narrow streets
Poplar-guards have a severe look.
The gardens and courtyards are covered,
Like a beautiful face with a veil -
Guarded by evil dogs,
Who prevent a stranger's entrance.
Oh, how their maidens are captivating,
As smells teasing saliva!
And every evening obsessively
I hasten to a teahouse like a thief.
Again sweet tunes.
I hear someone behind the wall.
Come into my lonely tent,
Shining with a pearl moon gleem.

* * *

The Sufis have grasped the essence of life,
Burning grass in flasks and crucibles.
As necessary as the breath for us to know
That I can love and am loved.
Each day is tortuous without her,
You are exhausted. Your shadow is blurred.
Love is the beginning of everything.
So, my spirit screams without sounds within me
And our hearts are broken.
You are the food, the house, and the blanket.
Please, Rumi, settle my grief and pain,
With your parables.

* * *

Oh, plane tree, my plane tree!
Your trunk and foliage are strong like armour.
Why am I not at your level?
Why am I not from your family?
Strong tea varies from water,
It can quench your thirst and cool heat.
A veil can be useful to me,
To come to you with the moon.
We do not need words because kisses
Will replace them in a stolen hour.
In that moment, I'll love you,
As if, for once, there are no tomorrows.
And a maid will sing her song behind a door,
While her mistress will be groaning softly.
And leaves and days will fly as a legend
Dancing silently over the plane tree.

Raushan Burkitbayeva-Nukenova

Turkestan

Eastern colors strike the eye.
Houses are close to each other like wagons.
Every third speaks Uzbek.
The azure room speckled with Arabic script.
All tandoor bakers and drovers are blacker than soot.
Bazar - a heated oven in the morning.
The sun mercilessly burns bald marks,
An open stall full of fabrics and dishes -
Is a cornucopia filled with goods.
A Sufi's crypt has been left to edify us.
Domes of mosques turn blue over the city.
When cooled under the arches,
I can hear whispers and calls to prayer.
Doves are mourning, eagles are darkened in the sky.
Tulips and poppies entraced like bloody battles.

The Heritage of Genghis Khan

Oh, night, a sister to hours of insomnia,
And sensitive sister of thoughts!
Fair and pointed reproaches
Disturb sleep until sunrise.
Memory as a harmful old woman
Reveals every secret of offense taken.
Devastation celebrates victory,
Dragging its tail amongst dusty boards.
As a sand-devil, he ran over the land,
Gardens, cities, were engulfed in flames!
Having turned into ashes
Anid ruined mind work and labor...
Heres a crazy horse cavalry again
Riding beyond the mountains.
At the heady song of soldiers
Filling the air with joy.
Thousands of Batyrs waisted.
On the field of battle in their saddles
And in the arms of sweet maidens.
They are singing,
Having been seduced by affection!
Their crimson cheeks are redder than poppies,
Reverential feathers are so gentle,
Once quarrels, feuds, and fights are forgotten.
Having dropped like an amorous arrow
The grand Kagan is in front of the crowd.
The herd then went to water

Along a strawberry path...
Fate is full of cheating trails, household words
And night mysteries, they say.
Oh, the moment of encounter,
You are short, and sweet,
as a shadow in forgotten dreams!
Guards sleep near the Khan's yurt,
And the moon is on patrol again.
While warrior respond to woman's requests,
That Love deeply conquers!
A new day calls for campaign!
Horseshoes and stirrups are clanking.
Seedlings mature near the sleepy river.
Seeds are floating, dancing in water.
And fires will be built somewhere nearby,
A strange voice captivated your ears.
And the clouds were eager for bloody battle,
A tired Khan sleeps in a burial mound.
Becaming immortal like the sun when he rises.
A living legend to the end of time!
Yet, his descendants remain passive.
Once-firm hands became soft...
Eyes are full of eastern languishing,
A proud body sits firmly in the saddle.
Everyone meets behind the Volga;
The mountains, on the docks, and in the village.

The Wormwood Wind

The tan on his bronze shoulders
Shimmers in a copper-glaze.
While memory is alive in the genes,
A passion for campaigns still hot! ...

27.12.2007

One fine day

I will light a leisurely fire
To burn my sorrows in it.
Thoughts mature as cherries and
Violet valleys.
Moon, playing ball by a dream,
Will break the fence of night
And being thrilled with flight
Will clink aside crystal hail.
A star will drop into my hand -
An unexpected gift.
And after long separation
A dashing hord soldier will wink.
As he circles me around a fire
Surrounded by sparkling swords.
Then he will give me a necklace.
As dazed yards calm down,
Like a coin accidentally dropped: shining
In the sand.
I know this mystical contour.
It is a polished vignette...

Aul*

My contemporary is gloomy, passive and lazy.
He is tied to a glass and a couch.
Where does this valiant Scythian spend the nights?
He has been completely captured by a screen.
Wasting an aimlessly received gift
And being satisfied by a bobtail flock
He laments fate and blends
nocturnal smells of alcohol
With old tobacco.
It is raining outside,
His wife is silent
Grandchildren are surfing the net.
And eyes are watery.
Everyone will be awakened by spring.
By the talking sounds of dombra.

*Aul - village in Turkic language

Raushan Burkitbayeva-Nukenova

The feast in the Aul

Conversations are leisurely conducted
Dombra song played aloud.
Today we are celebrating victory,
The feast will be held until morning.
A white canopy is over the yurt.
Stars are listening to speeches,
Many jokes and much fun.
Gifts will be given off the cuff.
Bowls are full of meat,
Camel milk is fernmenting with affection.
A libertine brother
Touches hips with his eyes.
The night is steaming over the red steppe,
Until shadows dropp on the grass.
Somebody is bustling near the oven,
Others are eating halva.
A gunman is drunk and has dropped out
Like an arrow from the quiver.
He is a prisoner of that girl's body,
And has forced her fortress into repost.

The Caspian sea

Foamy camel milk
Is playful and heady,
I just cannot breathe enough
Of this wonderful air!
And the roar of the waves
Sounds like a flying symphony,
Calling us to a round dance
On the far shore.
I will fly up like a seagull,
And hang like a cloud in the sky.
And I will drift
Like a sail on the blue.
And I'll be back
As a drawling and stringy song,
Or a drop of rain,
Playing in the grass.

Mangistau

There was a time when
The vast ocean raged here.
See the deposits of shells
Compacted in the plates?
Now, the restless wind
Sings in the pits.
It's a deceptive heath -
Under which there is a sea.
The rain makes scarves shaggy...
Oil flows up to the sky!
And gas burns like a landmine.
The archipelago promises
A glut of wealth.
Looking around glumly
A shepherd drives his flock
To another ravine.
Bulky and proud camels are calm,
Chewing thorns with relish.
In chalk caves,
That were one day pink,
another - snow-white
Saintly elders wait
Having steeped into legend.

Chimbulak

To I.Mikhalkov

In the river pistachio stones are
Shooting a glance at the doubtful daisies.
Although, their concerns will melt far away,
Like zephyrous clouds,
Poor creatures, there is no point to keep count them
It is like counting the foam sprays,
That play with ruby leaves.
Who will flirt with you?
When you become lenten and sobersides,
And indifferent pines hang over
Your bald and boring head?
You will be depressed. It's time to wake up,
And to revive uncombed grass from the top!

Raushan Burkitbayeva-Nukenova

Bayan-aul

The hills rise,
Like the girl's bust
Young girls are innocent and gentle.
Stones capturing their clouds.
The river will tell proverbs and legends.
This world is cramped, colorless, without love.
When hearts throb apart, it hurts.
Steppe winds smell of bitter wormwood,
lonely shadows sadly freeze.
Morose songs memory stores.
Tears rain-wash granite.
Melodies of happiness rush birds,
Soul lovers, like merging rivers.
Sweeping roads is a long story,
Borders, bridges, all opening for us.

Bayan-aul – Pavlodar.
29.06.2008

Berel

Mysterious signs of heaven
And sounds of cicadas and old strings.
Where did the Huns, Sakas,
Go? Those who left the ligatured s
cripts of sacral runes?
And like a gold vein,
Carefully hidden from the eyes,
In the valleys of the Altai mountains
Where eternity shines and frozen crusts
remain intact,
As well as the sacrificial stock of Argamak horses,
Where are acenaces undamaged?
The code of kinship is in our blood.
And feeling tired of the humdrum
You will find yourself in prophetic visions.
Through the howl of disturbed blizzards
You will make your way to the deserted camp
And hear the sounds of your heart –
It is a pendulum beating in your chest.
Stars are twinkling, summer is finishing.
And kui is born on the way.

Raushan Burkitbayeva-Nukenova

To Gennady Zil-u

The moon has risen like a Shaman's drum
And shines on the shaggy grass,
where the air is tough.
Having covered up friends' tracks
A wheezing deer has crossed the pass.
Velvet antlers branching like a bush,
And a night river silvering in them.
Leading the slaughter
A hand will cut them with a blunt hacksaw
Having cast a spell,
The river cried and deer twisted,
And tears stood in innocent eyes.
While a storm was coming to sweep barriers away
Like a sister escaping from captivity,
Going to the pass and shaking an orange mane
You threw stones and howled.
As red blood filled glasses,
And vodka was mixed into a drinking elixir.

13.11.2008

Escape

Clouds are thinning over the valley,
Where the mountain ranges warm their back.
Having waited a day in the heat,
moths are flying upwards
Aligning over the riverbank.
A cliff awakened from the loud roll call
Is keeping watch on night wandering in the dark.
Deep shadows are trembling in the gloomy water,
The risen moon is intentioned.
The day is dying, minute after minute.
The leaves are rustling covered by turmoil.
Hazardous this shine of a dagger.
A fugitive woman has run away
along hidden trails
As a shaggy fog above the river canvas
Gathers caravans in hot pursuit.
A memory lays a clever snare,
And everyone stubbornly remembers lost love.
Rain will sprinkle the doorstep,
 abandoned in a hurry,
While a silent star cries inconsolably.
Moths are flying to the light,
They hurry since called by friends.
Yet, forgotten anxieties have been
washed out by rain.
A wheel is spinning and roads are broken.

Raushan Burkitbayeva-Nukenova

Under the gentle warmth
of shimmering observations.
She fell asleep on my shoulder.
There is a house over the pass
where heaven thunders,
Fathers reproaches will thaw the drifts.
And a blurred pupil looks into eternity
While a tattered hook of old memories
Is heard as a native melody!
A round-backed old woman will tail her tears.
The swooped rain beats like a whip.
A restless grandson is kneading clay.

The Great Silk Way

The land of Seven Rivers remembers
A busy hum of dialects
And sultry southern Kazakhstan
Where a caravan of goods took its course.

It spread along the valley
By a clink of Roman glass.
The river trembles in the mirror
Due to lines of gentle silk.

Gold jewels are for
Dazzling beauties!
A Persian carpet woven
For overseas gifts.

Singing dunes will suddenly
Expose the inflected forms of amphora.
Both East and West are enchanted
By the flowering of miraged gardens!

Chapter 5

Tomyris (poem)

Great Steppe,
Nomadic expanses!
The Jungar mountains
Watch over the peace.
The herds are grazing
In the midday valleys.
River water
Is as clear as a tear.
Greatness and stillness!
Only there are too much waves -
The mighty Irtysh
Cuts space.

But what's happening? The steppe
Is torn apart by
Nomads strife
From Altai to the Caspian Sea!
Like the shadow of a great storm,
A herd of horses is
Running and sweeping
Tents and people...
Locks of gray feather grass
Are trailing.
A steppe-dweller will mourn
Her sons...

Raushan Burkitbayeva-Nukenova

In the spring
Scarlet poppies will open -
Where the blood of
Ancient Sakas was shed!
A tulip will become red...
Oh, steppe how bright,
Your spring dress is!
Being caressed by the sun,
Your view is great.
Yaik waters your
Battle grass.
A Scythian is sitting in the saddle
Like a glowering eagle
Guarding a flock of sheep.

And how many innocent people
Were killed here!
In the same way that wolves in winter
Tear apart a camel...
However, frenzied people
Might be a powerful force.
They might be like a tornado,
And as blind as a fire...

***

Assyria fell -
The lioness of the East.
It was broken by the onslaught
Of terrible force.
And Babylon
Is in turmoil,
Its population
Is aghast.
(And an elephant will dance with fear
When it is surrounded by wild bees!)
Wild hordes -
Are not brought to heel by swords,
As well as their iron
They are will and power!

Horse soldiers are moving.
The sun is beating down.
A steppe is shaken
By the kicks of horses.
Warriors are rushing irresistibly
Through the steppe vastness
Like black crows.
Lands and people -
Living down to the edge
Of the sacred Nile,
Will be conquered
By this mad force!

***

Wars, invasions,
Disasters,
Grief from losses
Madness.
A thousand-headed monster is crawling
And devouring everything in its way
Spreading panic and horror,
Death and oppression.
Turning the steppe into a wilderness:
Famine, devastation, depression -
While death waits for innocent people...

***

A lonely ranger
Is dragged along the road
Tired of adversity,
And abandoned by God...
He is distracted with grief,
Under the sun and in the rain...
There is no daughter with him -
Chief, what has happened to her?

Unhappy father,
Inconsolable Farzan,
The burial mound
You left on the steppe.

Zarina was called
A star of the East.
But fate was
Cruel with her -
It gave her a baby -
A needy daughter
Who drove Zarina
Into impenetrable night...
There is only clay there
And eternal sand,
Where the gentle Zarina's
Voice infolded in silence...

Now Farzan
Has got Tomyris!
Hard life fell into a baby's lot -
To live without a mother.
A steppe will replace her...
A horse will become a cradle,
A spear will be a toy...

***

Tomyris, Tomyris!
The queen of the Saka
Do not be angered by fate.
Though fate is a tigress.
You smite with your beauty
More than the Tien-Shan fir-tree!

How can I compare
A steppe gazelle with you?
Maybe leopards were taught by you
How to walk gracefully.

A star light was born…

***

Soft skin is more
Transparent than bridal veiling.
You extinguished
The flowers.
With the fire of flyaway braids
Still burning,
The blue of your eyes is
Like an expanse of sky.
You are a queen at daytime.
Who will be you tonight?
You will reject the pride,
Drive conventions away!
Like a flexible vine,
Without the queen's dresses -
You will anxiously refer yourself
To passionate embraces…

***

In the tent Tomyris
Was without dresses.
Night covered her
With a blanket.
Forgotting pride
Her proud lips
Were seeking answers to
Impassioned pleas!

Two shadows were
Merging in the tent.
A lamp was trembling
Like a ruby eye.
She stood still
In powerful arms.
She was not the queen -
But a prideless slave?..

And in the morning - in front of everybody
She was sharper than metal -
And inaccessible as rock!

I didn't seem to see a white seagull
I saw a maiden on the foamy waves.

In the soft water
Gray Balkhash
Is timidly caressing
The nude body.

Though, the waves embrace
The Queen in their arms -
Her soul is alone,
Dominations pursue her...
She weeps in secret,
Then again, she makes
A Queen of herself...

Who can she share
Her deep feeling with?
She is fated to sail alone
Like a lost boat.
And tears are running,
Dissolving in water...
Balkhash cannot help
The Queen with her troubles.

***

In the tent – alone,
A deeply hurt husband
Is falling into rage
Like a wounded lion.
Adultery by the Queen is
A bite from a snake.
No poison more terrible
For marriage bonds!

A queachy slave
Was in the tent
And made the fire of love
From a spark!
Is it a dream? One day
On a white horse
You threw down
Your challenge to me
For the first time...
And spirit trembled -
You blew away
My courage and force
By the tenderness of
A woman's heart!

Mighty Rustam is
A copper body hero -
Any warrior would be
Afraid of you!
But now the whisperers
Are amusing themselves
In secret -
You are a king without a throne,
And a husband without a wife!
And news is going round of
Rustam leaving
His royal house...

***

Cyrus was smart, handsome,
And strong.
He dreamed of conquering
The whole world!
"I will take over Egypt,
Babylon, and other countries", -
He thought.
Rustam, taking no notice of
Fated signs,
Stuck to him
With the detachment of Sakas.

Having mustered a shield
He hurries to take Babylon
From a royal Persian!
The tower of Babel -
Is a pointing finger.
The Persian is looking at you
With lust and risk.
Though it is high
And reaches the clouds
The royal eye is looking
Down on you.
Ingenious Cyrus -
Who can excel him? -
He has sent forward
The "wild" Sakas!

—   Forward to the death,
Attack them, Sakas!
It impossible to repel
Such attacks. -
Oh, commander,
The King of the Persians,
Babylon has been conquered,
And opened as a chest!

Persian stalwart -
Sanguinary soldier
Torments Mesopotamia,
Robs and crushes.

This region is not poor -
It's filthy rich!
The invader is possessed
With greed for gain

The valleys of the
Tigris, Euphrates are groaning:
  - Oh, Babylon
The epitome of depravity!
After the vinous nights
Piles of coins
Will make heavier
The chests of rich people!

However, jubilant Cyrus is greedy
The conquered world is
Narrow for him.
A greedy eye looks further,
And wanders unflinchingly
To the lands of the East...
A warrior's spirit
Does not meet prohibitions:
- Go to war against Massagetae!
- Against Massagetae!

***

Mysterious curtain
Falls rustling.
The evening is seen
In the waves of Balkhash...
A lonely swan is
Thrashing in the water
And trembling like a flag...
Maybe it is in trouble.
This strange dance of the bird is
Sorrowful and hot.

A wind is blowing away
A single cry.
It is beating with its tight wings
Against the crest of waves,
And the waves are spreading
A Funeral groan.
It has lost its baby swan,
The waves do not know about it.
Somewhere a group of swans
Echo in the sky.

Long-necked Swans
Was motionless
Like a question mark. -
Yet, waves are wavering,
Washing away bitter sorrows..

Tomyris is alone
Like a white swan.
Fast waves
Washing her tears.
All the troubles of the world were
Too great of a strain on her:
Cyrus captured her son
He is far away from her...

– Oh, Cyrus!
You are perfidious, treacherous and
Intoxicated by war!
Your worthless babble is ridiculous,
Haggling is somewhat out of place here!
Have you decided to ask
Incomparable Tomyris for marriage?
I'll tell you
You just made me laugh!

The steppe-dweller raised her eyebrows,
Audacity is in her eyes:
  - Are you murderous? Well,
I will quench this passion!
You took my son by deceit,
Lured him into captivity by guile.
I will not stop taking revenge and
Having revenge I will enjoy!

***

A plain without boundaries is
The Great Steppe!
Only the sun and the wind
Can possess you.
Unsophisticated and
Free people live here.
Effeminate Persians
Will not find the way there...

Death is waiting for the Persians
In the "bloody country"
Death from heat
Or from war.
  - Wild steppe,
Gardens do not bloom there,
I am tormented by thirst,
There is no water there!
It seems to me,
That I left Paradise,
When I was pathfinding
Into this bunt land.

Over there, beyond Jaxart,
Which is as sullen as a guard,
The nomads Yurts are
Like a mirage...
The arrows dig

Like black widows.
Sakas warriors are
High-spirited and skillful.
The patter of hoofs,
Acenaces in hand...
Their hearts ask:
Will it be my last fight?
Will I come back home?..

***

A queen's eyelids –
 Narrowed with rage.
Oh, angry lioness,
Your time has come!
It this not a rainstorm
Coming from the horizon -
Your Amazons have
Started the battle!
A head fell at Tomyris' feet.
Having sprinkled the grass
With a king blood.
Cyrus' head was
Put in a wineskin.
-   We have quenched your thirst!

***

The steppe has gladdened
In anticipation of peace:
Glorifying Tomyris who
Overcame Cyrus!
The Great Cyrus
Whose fame resounded.
Tomyris could take off his head
 In battle.
As the sun was overhead the steppe -
You shine alone,
Brightened with fame!

A steppe is free,
Like a wild flying horse.
Is your hand strong enough to curb and
Restrain a bridle?
There are many words
About the cunning and treachery of
Chiefs!
They have long been known
For their evil greed.
They cannot live together
In this free steppe.
Only a cruel enemy can
Pull them together,
Into one fist.

Do not wait for reconciliation
On these peaceful days:
Steppe chiefs
Torment each other!

***

The Great Steppe,
You are only dependent on the sun.
It would be great
If the tribes held together!

***

Tomyris is alone in the tent,
Like a pale moon.
The mirror is in the hand of the Queen -
She cannot fall asleep this night...
Catching her look in the mirror,
Her eyes are burning like the stars.
Her smile touching her lips,
Now they freeze and then will shudder...
She breathes out freshness,
Like a marvelous spring.
But when she raised her eyebrows,
To line a contour -
Noticeable wrinkles
Appeared round the temples...

The Queen's look is sorrow,
Well, her time goes quickly!
How long will light foot and
Agility serve her?
Or, maybe tomorrow she will sit
In the saddle,
Execrating everything.

***

We are keen on stars,
Words satisfy our ears,
But gold in our hands
Never warms us.
Uts look is cood,
And a soul loses warmth therein...

There was a time when everyone
Admired Rustam.
He had mature valor,
And called Tomyris his wife,
But her feelings have cooled off.

We always want to have something,
That we cannot possess.
Tell me!
Who values owned things?
We has only loses,
Being ready to suffer again!

— I'm sorry, Rustam,
For my treason -
The house of lies is
Like a captivity ...
Oh, spirits,
How can I move on?
I cannot make you alive...

***

Tomyris! Tomyris!
The Queen of the Sakas!
I pray for the power of spirits – Appear!
I cannot sleep at night.
Tomyris! Tomyris!
You are a steppe mistress!
My fire gives
A trail of sparks.
On your steppe
I can easily breathe!
Artemisia gives bitterness.
The song makes my heart sad
Gray feather grass wove
Like silver waves.

***

Your hair is red-hot.
Like a fire.
Your soldiers are resting at night.
Voicing -
Tomyris! Tomyris!
The night is finishing! Wake up!
The fire flame has gone out
Turn around!
When a new day comes,
As the spring flood,
Melting as a myth...
Time is like a handful of sand.
Heat is hammering at the temple,
Tomyris! Tomyris!
Step on the trail,
Burning fate!

***

A golden eagle is sailing through the sky,
Looking around the vast,
Majestic steppe
And silent mountains...
The sun is going on patrol
In its golden chariot.
Time slipped downhill
Since year one...

Raushan Burkitbayeva-Nukenova

The moon will shine at night,
Like embers in the hearth
Or a sad lamp
In the mournful hand...
On the ruins,
Where there are no bones
An archaeologist will find
A golden brooch...

***

Combs, rings, earrings,
Arrows, acenaces...
An ancestor drew signs
By a nib on the bowl!
A warrior in golden armors
Sleeps in a tomb...
Each work is
Worthy of a master!
Tigers and deer
Gold brooches,
Combs and jewelries
Run through the centuries.

There is no trace of those who
Possessed them,
Millions of fates are
Like sand in the desert.

Have wars or diseases
taken their lives?
Who will honor their memory
On the great funeral feast?

Where are you, our ancestors,
Huns, Scythians, Saks?
Argamak horses became the lines
In the legends.
Arrows were fired.
Acenaces are faded...
Poppies blush here
Like drops of blood...

***

The rumors flew
Over the ground
As the winds:
Awaken spirits
Sleeping for centuries!
The spirits of flown away and
Forgotten ancestors,
Now bother the living,
Like the wind bothers branches.
They come to the visions of
A deeply sleeping person
And fill the inner soul with force.

And perceived grandchildren
Stood in awe,
Having bent the knees.
Mistakes made our children
Who thirsted the words
Stretch their hands in question!

The shadows of our ancestors
Pass by like a long train -
Warriors, daring horsemen
Of old generations...
Their minds and souls
Flesh a secret veil
Having opened it for the living,
Accept them in peace
By your enlightened hearts.
Remember the steppe, eternal laws!
Stop wars and sorrow,
Life is a moment - not an eternity!
Let intelligence and
Heartiness be glorified forever!
To protect hearts from evil thoughts
Quickly turn your soul
Toward God, humans,!
If you hope for the best
You will not meet with pain,
Start the third millennium
With peace and love!

Chapter 6

Echo of war (poem)

Echo of war (poem)

June 22, 1941

Who said that the land does not moan,
When it bends under the weight of tanks?
They stick into land with tracks spreading smoke, and
Deal death by scoffing at remains.

Menacing hordes are burning the horizon
And covering it like a gray cloud.
Having thrown down deadly clusters,
They move at the front in columns.

Who can breathe by gassy flames?
Blood and smoke are in the hellish thick of war.
A sinister cross was on a banner,
Disturbing the sleep of a peaceful country.

Insidiously and without declaring war,
Fascists were coming: "Drang nach Osten".
There were bombings and bestial grins
Along the border - in every village.

"Farewell Motherland! Brest will never surrender! "
The border guards were killed in a battle.
"Sorry, Mom, your son will not come back!"
He will be a poppy in the feather-grass steppes.

Raushan Burkitbayeva-Nukenova

The Land grew yellow
Neither because of ripe and dense grain
Nor tight sheaves,
But because of mortar fire.
Steppe, you did not want such a harvest.
Your cultivators, your plowmen...
Went to the front as volunteers.
There was fighting from dawn to dusk,
Komsomol did not surrender the land to enemies.

And the huge country was rising, as one nation
To protect its sacred heritage.
It is impossible to forget those harsh years.
The Volga overflowed with blood.

***

You're standing naked by the river and laughing.
Clouds sprucing up your reflection.
A broiling day tired me,
Shadows were excitedly flowing.
And the terrible news of war suddenly struck
everyone dumb.
I will remember it forever -
The beauty of smooth curves,
The sweetness of mature peals
And June juicy rennet.
On this day a border guard is
Bound to be killed.
A signal flare trace was
Dying out … in the binoculars .

***

"Ferdinands", "Tigers" and "Panthers" ...
A gloomy General Guderian is
Looking through binoculars with an iron faith.
"To take over Moscow" is his evil plan.

The enemy has gathered unseen force
To extract the hearts from our chests.
Zhukov, Konev ... our compatriot, Panfilov,
Says: "There is no going back!"

And having closed with the enemy in agony,
They were defending Moscows approaches.
Our harsh climate was a severe distraction
For German tanks glowing in the blue.

But neither rain nor snow bore down the enemy,
People protected Moscow with their breasts.
Every citizen and all our troops defeated the enemy:
"We shall give our lives for Moscow!"

"Katyusha" defended our soldiers,
Foot troops were in a fire ring.
Everyone knew that our cause was good.
And the day would come and we would win!

Twenty-eight brave heroes,
Political commissar Klotchkov, Momysh-uly.

The Wormwood Wind

Let us remember those nameless warriors
standing without a word.
Mass graves are by the Vistula.

Raushan Burkitbayeva-Nukenova

Stalingrad requiem

It is not the sound of May thunder
Above our Mother-Volga River -
The sky wants to remember those who fell
Blushing like a fire line.

Bullets are flying as black hail,
The roar of Messerschmitt planes is in the sky -
A deadly battle rages over Stalingrad,
Blood is boiling in river crests.

For every building, for every passage
We paid with the young blood.
The boy, who did not know love
Was excitedly peppering the enemy
with a machine-gun.

It was a merciless street fight,
Tanks were spoiling to cross,
Our Motherland called to follow her,
We cannot forget those days.

Even a stern grandmother's brother
Remembered the war with tears in his eyes:
"We turned gray in Stalingrad
The earth was shaking under our feet".

Piles of corpses and a smell of burning...
We went all the way in the flames of hell
A Kazakh boy fought like a lion
Where millions of hearts became silent forever.

Mamayev Kurgan silently keeps
Secrets of the fallen and mothers' lamentations.
Clouds are floating over the Volga River
May thunder will remind us in a volley
of those batteries.

Grandparents see dreams of war,
They become deaf from explosions and cannonade,
And those soldiers fallen in Stalingrad
Had paid a great price for the life we have now.

Our glorious kin, venerable Jambul,
Inspired soldiers with songs,
There were the letters to him in a distant Aul,
His son was killed in the war.

And my father's brother did not come
Back from the bloody and terrible war.
Do not forget the fee they paid -
For the nightingales' songs and peace.

Raushan Burkitbayeva-Nukenova

War tides

Snow thaws…due to spring impassability
And heavy marshes of roads are everywhere
Heh, my little spade – you are my
faithful companion.
Your master feels chilly in the fire trench
And timely "commissar" one hundred grams
Are flowing like a gentle warmth.
Somewhere there, under the old cherry tree
They are waiting for letters sitting by the
pocked table.
Black-and-white pictures-twinkle,
We will keep your faces for ages.
They are writing letters - their revelations.
A political commissar with faint smile.
Was aware of all our secrets,
Opening a triangle at night.
Heh, post roads-counter roads ,
Don't burn letters in the oven

They wait for news, having chilled in the trenches,
Wait for news in the villages and hospitals.
Having patched wounds with a song,
They spoil for a fight, work at machines,
sit and in fields!

Approaching the victorious marches, and
Forgetting about fatigue and fear.

They become wiser and older
When raising the flag on the Reichstag.

You have raised our Victory Banner,
Rakhimzhan Koshkarbaev, our hero!
Letters from war can tell us,
How they lived during war.

***

Stalingrad stood in ruins,
Having swept the enemy away.
Blockaded Leningrad shone
Like an unbroken needle.

Such people cannot be conquered,
Mark this well, Fritz!
Do not reopen wounds.
You should not have gone Eastward.

Our cities are coming to life,
And rye has matured in the fields.
Peace has conquered forever
Do not worry soldiers.

Raushan Burkitbayeva-Nukenova

***

Do you remember that terrible bombing and
The heart-rending sound of alarm,
Daydreams about fried potatoes
And dates under the lilacs?

Never kissed boys and
Never loved girls,
Are taken out of the medical battalion
As boarded shutters.

Having been committed to earth ...
The Motherland
Thry keep secrets behind tired faces.
And praying for the dead
during shared funeral feasts,
Mourning became rain and melted snow.

Fellow and brother soldiers
Come into our visions and knock at windows.
They stretch as branches in an embrace,
And lie as flowers beneath our feet.

"He has gone missing"- a mother is mourning.
My child, taken away by the war.
Where shall I find him? Personal troubles
Made manifest by the Berlin Wall

And hopes melt everywhere.
They wait by quenching grief with tears.
And carefully make a bed with withered flowers.

It is not the cry of rain – but the voices
Crying from the sky.
Their stripes resplendent .
They do not forget the war.

The soldiers fallen in the fields.
Both a German mother and a Russian mother -
Asked for their children's return
When poplars burnt as a candle.

Untold losses ...
And grief from murdered dreams.
No longer knocking at your door,
There will be no joyful meetings.

A mother does not accept excuses.
Sounds of knitting cannot
Reduce an open wound.
The Madonna's eyes look through window frames

Raushan Burkitbayeva-Nukenova

***

A sanitary train is travelling East,
Having recorded the losses on a battle sheet.
Ah, tried soldier, your life hangs in the balance.
While surgeons hold a scalpel
twenty-four hours a day.

A lamp is gloomily on the table.
A heaven-born Aesculapius will create a miracle.
And an enemy splinter extracted in silence.
Allows a brave soldier to hurry on vacation.

A sanitary train is a cradle across roads
It rocks a soldier to prevent him from chilling.
Cover him, sister. Where is his coat?
Outside his window a blizzard sings its song
like a mother.

***

Tons of porridge and borscht -
It is a field kitchen!
It works cheerfully
Under the shelter of a cloak.

A soldier had been waiting for
You since morning
When he rested by the fire,
Having forgotten about crazy death.

Boiling water instead of tea.
While hearing friendly spoons clatter.
Taking no notice of inconvenience,
A trooper chews a spring onion.

Let's kiss goodbye!
Will we meet again or not?
Send a message, mate!
Cooking dinner, chef!

So, brewed porridge!
Fritz skedaddle home.
And by scatterings quadrille
Tucked into a thick soup.

Here's tasty porridge!
Let fritz skedaddle home.
And within the sounds of our quadrille
Soldiers are eating thick borsch.

From one halt to another,
Do not stint rations, or fate.
We warmed with hope,
Since Victory Day is close!

***

An actor at the front-line is more than an actor!
Artillery salvo of shells...
And I pounded your accordion,
Into a waltz without clothes.

A soldier's shirt fits well,
And boots are shined with a brush!
The commander is running to an anti-aircraft gunner,
Do not get him into trouble, a stretched line.

And heels are firmly dancing,
Their rhythm sounding like a squall wind.
(Has Intelligence made progress?)
Our eyes are glowing and clear.
At tea cooling in a table glass.

Nightingales are calling us to restoration,
Where grapes become glossy over the vine.
War is ending, and the concert is over.
Then comes a time of storms.

Artists enlivened a bloody day,
Singing songs within the site of fire.
Fate was waiting for a soldier near the crossing.
Actors proudly wear their medals.

My wounds begin to trouble me, as the years go by.
Grandfather tells his grandson: "Walk at my back!"
That is not a blizzard howling in the steppe,
These are the moans of soldiers at night.

A grandfather is exposing his back,
A chubby toddler is groaning.
Where are my countrymen? They lie in foreign ground
Like a black cargo.

A grandfather crawled and walked
Over half of the land.
He went all out to win.
A surgeon accurately sutured the wounded,
Mopping clammy sweat from his face.

He is a war hero,
However he does not display this fact,
His medals shine like stars.
In May, he looks for brother soldiers.
Those fellows who faced death a hundred times.

Unconsciousness

This is not a chorus of wolves in the steppe,
These are voices of fallen soldiers
Over the peaceful Volga.
Who is wheezing
Having frozen on a viscous and overly long note.

Being crushed with gray snow,
Piles of chips and bricks.
Had he forgotten survival skills
In years among neon nights?

The defender, gallant soldier!
One of the ranks who ascended skyward.
Your coat still has marshal medals
 Ever protected from covetous eyes.

Tell me, who is dancing in pain?
They fell in open fields.
Spring will bring them flowers.
Like them, we must remember everything too.

Recall a fathers' feats in arms
Not only on Victory Day
They leapt into the battle for the sake
of our Motherland,
Their coats shot with lead...

Raushan Burkitbayeva-Nukenova

***

It is not a dream, but a waking nightmare,
Youths excite Moscow.
Terrorists, fascists, skinheads...
Are you the haeres of glorious victory?

Brown fog of plagues -
Plaid hcad games. A fraud
Threatening soul and guts.
As deadly explosions detonating in a subway.

From the thick of a dormant alley -
A crowd of skinheads
Crawled in Moscow like a black widow
Blackening with Nazi swastikas.

Criminal Petersburg. Well, it can't get any worse...
Is it true that everyone forgot the war?
Russia! Is your youth blind?
Weeds, weeds, weeds...
Amid a brown muddy river.

***

In the dust of a sheeted road,
At an inaccessible height
Solders rest
Among lines of obelisks to beauty.

Spots and patterns have grown dim
On colorful dresses over the years.
However, sisters will wear them in villages.
Although, an old man saddened at a death letter.

He was drinking ... feeling sorry for that day
When a fascist had not cut his life.
Where is your pride, scarlet women?
You are standing by the post at night?

They sell themselves, bitches.
And tomorrow they will sell their country.
Ah, if the old man had united hands.
Instead of pointlessly wandering.

What kind of defense are you talking about?
The minister of trade sells lands,
Having diamond like a crown,
The war is forgotten, a lesson for all woes.

The elderly will die,
Leaving behind conscience, pain and fear.
Willows by the river will mourn
Those fallen in battle and in the lines.

And who will say, as formerly,
In such unforgettable years:
"I have the honor!"
Sorry, soldier.

Raushan Burkitbayeva-Nukenova

The solder's star burns
In scary light from the ceiling
Shrapnel is flying howling,
All night long, a regimental son is fighting,
Being wrapped in a coat.

It has patches all over it,
And shabby cloth
It embodies old roads
Having become old long ago.

A soldier is going to rest,
In order to fight through the night,
As seagulls fly over the river,
And a daughter is softly sighing.

The war ended for a long time ago.
Yet, its fragments still crush our dreams.
Victorious spring
Please revive all of us.

A deep trench is like a moat.
A soldier has frozen with a bayonet on his cheek.
"Do not retreat!" - The order is severe.
"There is no earth over the river!".

A bloody and smoky dawn
Has covered Stalingrad.
Two hundred days and nights in a row -
We feel Hell on Earth.

The Wormwood Wind

A tank is again creaking over the trench
While death is rumbling in a dance.
Nurken Abdirov rushes into battle,
Throwing weapons in a whirl.

And "Tigers" in strong armor
Have surrendered themselves.
But it is a ruthless trap.
Snow is red over their knees.

The mound has become a magnetic hill
Where a fascist left his tank.
Our hero went through like a hurricane,
Drawing a noose.

Yet, lilacs dropped over the trench
Like a sister
Our enemy is troubled until morning,
The city is like a shadow.

Every block of houses, every building -
Looks like a fortress and a threatening wall.
The maternity hospital is completely closed
It is in a line fighting for life.

And among the explosions and fire -
The baby's cry is like a call.
He claims the right of day.
A ditch is buzzing in delight.

Raushan Burkitbayeva-Nukenova

Proud Stalingrad is meeting
A child of war.
Ruslanova was singing
While they were clearing mines

"Valenki" saved a soldier
Who was dreaming of spring.
And he did not grudge the lead,
As light in the window was summoned.

A night sky guards the trench,
It is grassed over!
A sleepless star trembles
Over a peaceful street.

Once again a grey-headed February is sad
And our Motherland looks into the distance
Through a gloom laden fire.

Mamayev Kurgan will keep
Soldiers' hearts.
The sainted fire of those days still burns.
And grandchildren arukk have their father's eyes.

It is not frequent to see a front-line soldier
In streams of people.
A son has clung to the earth
Picking up handfuls of soil.

Fighters are in the trench,
It is their earth-house.
They are at home, like singing starlings.
Rejoicing in their memory of their sacred grandfathers.

A younger grandson has become a general,
He is a threat to thieves.
Oh, how proud would his father be!
His eyes running with hundred-gram tears .

Oh, Mother Volga,
The feather grass is sad.
Curled ears of wheat,
Came to the trench.

Years and centuries will pass.
And victorious May will come.
Clouds will guard the gray Mamayev Kurgan
Through groans.

Once again poppy colours will be spread
Like an unfading fire,
As memory of those sacred years,
Live inside it forever!

Raushan Burkitbayeva-Nukenova

***

Snow melts and your number is melting,
Our Second World War veterans.
Cranes fly to the south,
At news of these fated fires.

And the flame of Eternal Glory does not diminish,
Human rivees do not dry.
Swearing an oath-communion,
We shall keep this feat through ages!

To L.Yu. Grishu

Booms of cannonade never trail away
In severe and frosted silences.
Defenders of Moscow and Stalingrad
You fell involuntarily in battle.

Those who in tanks, planes and blindages
Fought, in their generation, throughout the night
For every house and every village.
A reality beyond movies and mirages.

Souls are in stasis because of relatives killed,
But indifference makes pain greater.
And looking at the carelessness of youth,
The very fate of our land is questioned!

You come to blows,
As war and disaster tempered your spirits.
Yet, we are ready to help everyone extinguish fires,
And tirelessly plant new gardens.

Duty, honor, integrity are in your blood from birth,
The christening of steely generations from
those times of war!

***

As light as a dying spark
Is the coat a young man.
His uncle is sewing it
Bending over his machine.

A fashion placket, strap and collar...
Lenya was swaggering in a coat!
The war has come to a picturesque town.
Although, ignoble enemies killed our relatives.
He decided to live.
Amid fear and deception.
A coat that was taken from a trembling mother,
Standing at a grave pit,
A traitor had hidden in the closet.
But payback time will come for the killer.
And pain kill him lik lead in soldier's chest.
But, it does not decrease.
And in a hospital room
He writes prose and poetry,
Distilling memories of childhood and
Front-line friends.
Ironically, this farewell greeting,
Touches the wounded fate...

Victory

A brooch of opulent sunshine
Glimmered festively over the village!
The clanking sounds of orders and medals for
Warriors returned from abroad.
And the orchestra brass spills
Down serenaded streets.
Where the tears of women revived life
Through happy chores
And the fuss of awakening children.
How spring reacts to new moments,
Instantly transformed the light of day.
The world flushed with joyful fun
As a grandfather was quietly crying.

Raushan Burkitbayeva-Nukenova

Inaguration of the monument to Aliya Moldagulova

You were neither a bride nor a wife,
At incomplete nineteen you were assumed into heaven.
And in May Victorious Spring
You stepped upon a pedestal in our homeland.
Dzhigits returning from the battlefield,
Brought flowes to you in their arms.
Uct, the years do not respect them, and they, unlike you,
Are quiting the ranks.
You alone are coaeval with the war generation ...
Whose aim was certain.
From native land and ruined villages
You put pressure on enemies when seeing them in the snow,
You raised soldiers to the attack
And led the way.
Your voice rang when it was cold and dark:
Otan Ushin! - You led a platoon to the attack.
And afterwards you read them Jambul,
About the pride of an old man from the steppe.
While night was heated by the fires of your native village,
As the forest was dozing and the river was sleepy.
How sweet that dream in this impenetrable hell,
White snow will cover a trench,
But hope will blossom again in our souls
In the form of a massage from Blockaded Leningrad!
This forest will remember such growlings of war
As well as your voice, and your calls in the night.
Young soldiers were ready to attack,

The Wormwood Wind

And red calico twisted over the trench!
You came back to our homeland as a legend.
Crowned with heroic stars.
Yout tan is bronze, and locks are copper.
You came to the feast under a blanket
You were niether a bride nor a wife ...
And, as if in the betashar ceremony,
You showed your face to the crowd,
Young and old incline their heads in highest regard.

The sky brought tears to the clouds.
Your Kobda is more tansparent than tears.
Having decorated the town, you will never leave us.
You will always protect us!

Aktobe 23.09.2005

Chapter 7

At the end of the day

***

The grapes of doubt swelled with tears,
Rain beating against the window.
Castles are collapsing in the air,
A deserted dock is languishing .
Where are the ships and courageous captains?
A parrot-talker is sleeping.
Only people are sleek and formidable.
Where are you, searchers through runes?
Who will revive these stones with prayers
And decode lost words?
Only the steppe grass cries
Having admired terrible battles.
Its feather grass becoming gray from graves,
Our poppies are brighter than flame.
Who will voluntarily releases the reins
And saddled the horse?
A minaret grows deaf in the steppe
Like an arrow directed to God,
Battle cries call to the road
By a ring of worn coins!

Breach

A tearful autumn has retreated
Replaced by quiet, although punctual, snow.
As it desperately covered windows
With paper – uet, a spooky, artful, fire ignited.
He has gone, though she begged him to stay.
She even threatened to take their children away.
But, love is the main reason and measure!
They are drifting apart...

On the swarthy face

There is a shadow of embarrassment
On your swarthy face.
My appearance has
Excited you.
And you are, as a boy in love,
Flying - and so enthusiastically
Singing and talking.
It is funny to
Watch all this.
But feelings do not want
To give me freedom.
I know that this is an
Exciteable minute.
When you're gone,
It will be empty and obscure.

***

Snow stubbornly falls at our feet
Covering a slush road.
Someone is working over there –
In the stellar distances,
To make us cleaner and taller than we are!

Raushan Burkitbayeva-Nukenova

To Z. And M. Kakimzhanovs

Snow falls from the sky in a silent, hopeless and
Slow manner, as if it were a slow motion picture...
And something long-forgotten is awakening,
Charm has enveloped the city and the forest.
A fragile and transporent templet of snowflakes
Will melt from warmth and taught lips
And leave a tart taste of regret.
Time, impermanence, rushing into the abyss of years.
Yet, our city will be cleaner and kinder,
As in a black-and-white movie.
And the smell of mint herbs will thicken in bottles,
And dusty roads will settle like an old wine.

***

Wind tears off September leaves
Like pages from a calendar.
Autumn generously covers the table.
A shy birch has such a graceful trunk!
Waves polish the amber stones.
September evening burns quietly.
Memory will grind the faces of bright days.
Your footprints will melt on the sand.

To friends

If you were king
Of a great country, and
Lived in a luxurious palace
You would be lonely
Without friends...
You could raise
With invisibles a graceless cup,
Having filled it with champagne!
Their happy faces are
Above all treasures!
I can share my sadness
And joy with them.
My eyes aspire to you
As to the bright sun.
I miss them,
Oh, how I love them!
And every meeting gives us
Wonderful moments,
And grants discoveries like
A river of pearls.
It is revelation
Or a moment of inspiration,
When a friend's hand
Touches you.

Raushan Burkitbayeva-Nukenova

***

The moon looks through my window
Like a question-mark all night long
Promising insomnia.
Notes are flowing into the dew.
Why do you torture me?
Whenever I relax -
You start to blaze again.
You beat like showers against walls and
Sending me a basket of flowers.
You follow me like a shadow.
Our meetings and dreams are destined
To be shared by separation.
Because love is crowned with eternal torment,
A river - with trembling bridges.
The stars shine out of the darkness
Like embers in a stove.
God created women from the ashe,
Sticking stems into the sky.

03.01.2009

The Wormwood Wind

***

The sun freezes on the window frame,
Sliding slowly at the slant.
Evening is walking through quite yards
Imprinting leaves into the sand.
A tree naps having sloped forwards.
And the phone is treacherously silent.
Autumn was hanging at our parting,
Wrapped in my gifted scarf.
Winter is coming and looking cold
As a jealous mistress
And snow is flying down from heaven
Like a tousled thread.
Twilight is thickening over the river.
So, arm yourself with patience until the spring.
Allowing sadness to melt like a silent candle,
While warbled calls burst into dreams!

7.12.2008

Raushan Burkitbayeva-Nukenova

Burning candle

There is a burning candle in silent stillness,
Although joy is not hurrying towards me,
And this night seems to be eternal-
As my hope is moving away.

Having gathered pains, I'll leave hastily.
Love will go out like this candle.
Yet, parting with you will balm my aches,
I'm tired to wait for my leading role!

Like a soaring bird high in the sky
I'll run away from you - far away.
You needn't tame me,
Since, you will start all over again.

Not every key unlocks the lock,
Once being broken, my bow has gone silent.
The same as a violin is silent without the violinist,
Candles die without the light of love.

And wax is dripping like tears,
While, soul is cry for falling in love with you.
But you have not learnt the beauty of love,
Having burnt to the end, I'll go into darkness...

Friend's call

To Yu. Koshkin

Life is playing hide and seek with me.
Maybe I've forgotten something somewhere.
Days run away without looking back,
And my passion is scattered like ash.
An idea will spin flashing
Over the block of houses
And it floats out turning cold,
In opposition to well-fed brains.
Yet, living in different dimensions
Under, it would seem, one roof
Two centuries, three generations,
No longer hear each other.
Juicy cherries were ripe,
I picked them bythe handful in our garden.
And now I'm a stranger at this party,
I'll move into the shade when get tired.
Lilacs will be cut to make bouquets -
Days are indifferent to old people.
Newspapers will ruffle like leaves.
Only stumps are left from pillars.
While my town is poisoned by smog
Tell me what you're breathing with today?
I will sing an octave higher
Hurrying to the journey in the morning.

Raushan Burkitbayeva-Nukenova

On the outskirts of the day

Poems don't come easy,
And there is more sadness than laziness.
Days apply strokes to the skin
And shades thicken under pine trees.
It's not easy to go upwards,
I am short of breath at every step.
The river edge will get frozen,
Doubts narrow the ice-hole.
The load of unforgiven offenses knock down,
A crying child anguishes at night.
North winds are fierce and angry,
As a mosquito buzzing over the river.
Reckless and easiness have left.
Every dawn of crimson cheeks gets pale.
While garden footpaths become overgrown with moss,
And the vast steppe is numb.
Herds of clouds have come down from the mountains,
Horses are harnessed for hunting.
The huntsman will meet gray-haired experts.
I'm out of range - my cell phone is off.
I break a link with our earth
I leave like a pilgrim in the desert.
Where stars' inextricably ligature
Into an intensity of passions uncooled.
I'm light like a yogi in prostration.
There is a smell of herbs, wicker.
There are no convenineces of civilization.

And rivers are clear like a tear.
There is a soul in every bush.
Handfuls of stars sparkle with ash.
There is a cleanness of otherworldly acoustics.
There is a hot soup-shulyum in the pot.
Night will squat nearby, curing with a miraculous potion,
You will spread your wings like strands,
lifting them up gently
Above cares burdening your shoulders.
Our crescent is carved like the brand mark of ancestors
My heart is moans like a vibrating string.
And dawn advancing in a snowstorm which sweeps aside
All the doubts of the moon.

01.12.2008

Raushan Burkitbayeva-Nukenova

Mystery of Mona Lisa

Madly in love,
Proud, gentle.
Hardened in labour,
Fragile, snowy.
Now sultry, passionate,
Then serene.
Beautiful girlfriend,
Boundless joy!
You strike men
With just your look
And you walk boldly
Towards your goal.
Beneath your heart you wear
The mystery of centuries ...
Your smile will be inherited by children.

In transparent worlds

In ghostly distances,
In transparent worlds
Clouds have melted -
The wind blew someone's ash ...
Like running threads
Through the ring of a vertebra.
Dim light
Will extinguish the hand of death.
Farewell, my body,
I'm turning into a mirage.
I'm a ghost, I'm haze
In transparent worlds.

Raushan Burkitbayeva-Nukenova

Moonlight snow

To K. Gulnar

On the shaky border of
A birthday
In anticipation of
An ice drift.
I know,
You will again
leave me
With rays of lightning
Before the sunrise.
Oh, so thin,
Is this filigree-fast
Of severe ice
As it edges to the shore!
You are so thirsty for heat
But a series of days
Will spin you
Hysterically.
And moonlit snow
Like good news,
From cherished orbits
Will pirify, like white light ...
Once again, we are together,
Darling, you're here!
The moonlight snow is dancing!
There is a light of love and forgiveness...

In winter

To K. Jaksan

As though in a punitive shirt
The willow sleeps dutifully under snowdrifts.
While in a sagging fur hat
The post is on duty on a far hill.
An undisturbed peace
Reigns around over the white steppe
And over an abandoned river
Mist rattles with an iron chain.
A shadow of chilled fir trees
Seems like a fresco across shouldered snowflakes.
Yet, hiding its feet from blizzards,
The aspen is trembling from the chill.
Birches are whitening, ghostly
In the frosty forest temple.
And from the shackles of harsh prose
Word-blizzards are flying in a solid veil.
Although, frost keeps control of everything.
Sadness rules in the forgotten kingdom,
Where birds are freezing in open fields.
And a resistant agaric saves power.
A hungry wolf argues with the moon,
As a cat calms near a hot stove.
And a bitterly cold wind gives birth to a blank verse.

Raushan Burkitbayeva-Nukenova

Flickering snow...

Blinded with the whiteness
        Of a January morning!
So solemnly
        A fully dressed day comes in.
Shimmering snow,
        Is like a powdered mirror.
There is a lush shade
        Of clapping wigs.
While ermine mantles
        Shelter slopes,
Nature freezes
        In the hushed garden.
Because superstitious feaes
        Give bows
We are in irredeemable debt
        Before the future,
This day, this light,
        This snow, these distances...
Are given freely to us
        By a generous hand,
But we have foolishly
        lost our lot,
And we leave humbly
        For our last days of rest.
Stray thoughts
        Walk in a snowstorm.

There is scattered frost -
               In my hair.
Icy silence of
               A winter bed.
And there are disturbing notes -
               In steel voices.
And rhymes and music are composed
               Of genius
 Polishing obsessively
               With graceful verse.
And dazzling moments
               Of winged birth.
Fly at midnight
               As shimmering snow
Is quiet ...

12.12.2008

Raushan Burkitbayeva-Nukenova

Poem – and – me

My persistent lines
Are flying like telegrams through a dream.
They are accurate like monograms -
The farewell lessons of destiny.
They are sad with snowdrifts
Together with flying rains.
Previous and upcoming poems
Follow our steps.
They, like a mass, airborne, slurry,
Stand as pillars in a frosty battle.
And gleam like lanterns along future routes,
And wait patiently in a notebook.
When insomnia torments,
They will quietly enter my soul.
And vocalize my sadness with a line,
And teach appreciative moments,
I will not reduce their magic.

Imminence

Oh, if I put all my strength into tenderness,
Then like the sun I'll melt the ice of separation.
You'll learn the vastness of my love.
I hasten towards your canoe on the far shore!

***

Leaves are rustling underfoot -
Like garlands of broken phrases
This harsh life is right -
And I will forget my pain - and you.

Raushan Burkitbayeva-Nukenova

Autumn story

From the smoky garden -
Wrapped in a warm evening,
Through cast-iron fences
Autumn is moving forward.
Rain tortured by colds
Is trotting obediently after it.
The day with short amplitude
Is waiting for a phonecall in stuffy apartments.
It will disappear in the curls of a willow
Like a wind gusting with farewell themes.
My evening is quiet, empty.
On the glass a maple leaf has flattened
like a fingerprint.
There is a pair of kid gloves,
Forgotten by a new admirer...

26.11.2008

To Ilfa

A carousing, fierce, wind has covered
The ice hole with fragile ice.
In this gloom the hopeless lines of
A sad song disturb the moon.
My soul grows cold from sorrow,
And the days are compressed like a vise.
There is a slim outline of faded enamel,
Elegant thumbs ...
Once remembered and admired,
Yet, the glass is overturned accidentally.
Against the muffled sounds of a piano.
And cooled raspberry tea ...
My sister left for Denmark
Flocks of birds are stretching to the south.
And there are apples in the parcel as a message from
The heart of the mountains
And the warmth of our hands.

Raushan Burkitbayeva-Nukenova

Shoemaker

There is a shoemakers booth at a crossroads,
A philosopher has a handful of fresh news.
Maybe he will tell us where to find happiness?
There are thousands of destinies, hundreds of roads,
There is a tired shoe laying on the shelf.
He cheers us with a funny joke -
He heals our souls like Dr. Doolittle.
The arch support is broken and the heel is too quick,
And the boot slider is broken thereabouts.
These boots have come off taps,
They are laying sick on a bed.
Yet, for all the tricks of capricious fashion
The shoemaker looks with a smirk and
Again clutching a nail after initial revisions,
Starts hammering, frowning.
Where is your way walking?
Is your wallet thin or thick? -
Having a look at those shoes, he will understand
When necessary, in silence, he will sew on a patch.
A local shoemaker is a sage and a philosopher,

Quayside of day-dreams

In the tram, fall has driven everyone to steamy windows
And quiet asleep.
And like shots of an old movie
 Frosty houses are floating.
- Tell to us who will pay rent?
- And where the owner is? - He's crazy.
Houses have been taken away.
Princesses have left their habitual nests.
House has been converted into shared apartments.
Akthough, courtiers keep their manners, their etiquette.
They are still gentle with their cousins.
Yet, Russia is no longer in our world.
The brilliance of its era will not return,
The greatness of Russia, the royal house,
Openwork scarves, fans, sighs.
Holds a sadness for the past.
Exiles are strangers with a cruel fate.
Their roots remain among birches
As messengers of a silver time
They seriously hope to return to their dream.
A taxi takes them from a birthday party
Along the labyrinth of Parisian streets.
- Madam, here is your change - merci, merci!
- I'll drive you to the entrance - even closer.
- In Russia – there is a house, a helpful servant.
He is waiting for me, - night starching snow
It seepes onto the roads, backstreets.

- Life was more comfortable and freer then!
Palaces keep (Sheremetevs', Yusupovs')
the Fontanka's banks.
Winter in Paris is like our homeland summer -
 Dull rains and Summer Gardens.
You're free in your memoirs.
And every evening – there is just a backwards look.
They say Turgenev is a Prisoner of Pauline Viardot's spell.
You should not stir up that "Noble Nest".
The road winds like Duncan's scarf.
The faithful grey sphinx is waiting at the threshold!
The aging Tatarian is sweeping their yards.

Piece of poetry

A branch has swollen with sticky buds,
And there is a smell of spring in the air.
A sheet speckled with script lines
Is thrown away by a greedy hand.
Veins are swollen at the back of the head -
There is a pursing of convulsive lips.
And I'm pierced as if by a fork
The space between spheres, the invisible cube.
And a weak-willed thought is lagging
Behind a hypnotic bridge.
Suddenly, turning into a new song
And then it will become a hit.
Like a glassblower, I'm playing with fire.
I can resurrect, burn.
But losing this cherished thought,
I cannot smolder without thinking.

Raushan Burkitbayeva-Nukenova

Confession of Casanova

You'll remember the tart taste of wine
And deception, but yet you'll forgive.
Distances cost a pretty penny.
And playful Paris is farther and farther.
And more and more seldom women of
Easy virtue break hopes, hearts.
And the houses of Amsterdam
screwed up their features,
Guarding men on the porch.
And wives are worried at guessing,
And wash away lipstick through sobs.
There is a mystery flickering in every kiss.
But, you will find truth in someones eyes ...
At night imaginations are excited by
Silhouettes of past women.
Michel and Aspasia beckon again.
Casanova is hurrying to the temple of God.

On the steppe

The snowstorm sweeps the road.
There is a hoarse-roar from the motor.
Melancholy is camping on our doorstep.
Saksaul is burning in the stove.
The yurta's chest keeps heat,
Boiling broth is steaming.
We are guarded by severe frost.
While a medallion is ringing like silver.
Agile hands are rolling the elastic dough
And in the oven, passionate shoots
of flame sing like a song
Of revived night.
Bracelets caress the wrist
And the polished figure is elegant.
Dombra is bursting with happiness,
The red-hot cooking pot is trembling.
Yet, you are looking away embarrassed,
Dishing up sorpa.
A man in love is persistent,
Bold and hot is his kiss.
The kettle is hissing threateningly,
Our hot oven is buzzing.
Our flared-up willow is sparking,
And an unnecessary conversation will subside.
Having screwed up the shivering cold.
Drinking flavours like a dog.
Seized by hot breath ...

Raushan Burkitbayeva-Nukenova

The East famously lifts the Sun.
And morning will walk across the snowdrifts,
A mound gives off smoke.
The steppe is jealous of its chill.
Our fire is taming the snowstorm.

29.11.2008

---

sorpa – soup, broth (Kaz.)

To Yerzhan and Yerlan

My son has grown up imperceptibly,
A sprig straining after light.
The first bouquet of red roses.
A storm of failures and victories.
And a troubled peace,
The moon disc is broken by sadness.
You are beckoned by a park across the river -
An annoying song.
There is the joy of great changes,
There are hundreds of ideas and methods!
Bitterness of losses and betrayals,
And a volcanic boom of lines ...
And, reflecting in the river,
our house sails like a caravel.
There are slender pines in your scarf,
There is a pond edged with ice.
A faithful dog is waiting at the door,
Your eternal twin - shadow.
You dream is roaming until dawn.
In a day marked by the sun!

Raushan Burkitbayeva-Nukenova

***

My children are my continuation,
Two reliable strong wings.
My songs are my salvation,
Like a clean and bright prayer
That always saved me from trouble.

To the village!

To Tatiana

The city shrank like a burnt fell
Billowing rooftops and bridges,
Suffocating in the carbon monoxide smoke.
In that hellish inferno, you are perishing.
In the dusty vessels of narrow streets -
There is an engine roar of cool cars ...
Let my grandson grow among birds and chickens
Like a ball bouncing up to the heights.
Where quails prowl,
Where nightingales sing all night,
Pine and fir trees exhale fragrance,
Cows chew cud and cake.
Therem on the cart yoked to the colt,
Grandfather holds a substantial way of hay.
Although, even diaper cloth is warmed in the sun.
The moon pales like mercury.
Over there stars fall on the palm,
Mists roam across the river.
And you spoon yellow cream in cans
In handfuls.
I was there often in my childhood,
Catching dragonflies in my net
And dozed in the cradling mountain crossing,
Now, I'll take my grandson out of town!

To my grandchildren

To Aibar, Aisultan and Mikaela Merei

Scattered pages of poems
Will be gathered by me together in one chapter.
Caught in flocks like birds calling
And I'll go after them.
My tattered dreams will strain obediently after me.
And my grandchildren will believe naively -
That I'll retire until spring.
With a shabby book in bed,
Yet, when grouses bell,
Hear me in the snowstorm!
At the swollen crying door.
Rocking stars in the lunar cradle - I'll sing a lullaby.
And melting like a hoarsen icicle - I'll stand in the corner.
It's impossible to outargue the falling rain,
There is sadness on the windows, like mica.
All our life is a passing moment!
Snow will melt without a trace.
But the light of my distant cyes
And the mischief of steppe rivulets
Will be seen by my sons more than once
Through the whims of a little girl.

The Wormwood Wind

***

Accompanied by the moon
Heavenly sonata sounds.
While night is seized in inspiration,
And cherry trees get thick with ripening dreams.

Accompanied by the moon
From unimaginable and distant heights
Snow and sad light flow
Piercing the strata of silence.

Accompanied by the moon
Our twin like a lunatic,
Strides boldly on a tightrope -
There, all problems are solved.

Accompanied by the moon
We have shelter- find peace.
Tired of sufferings and waiting, we leave.
We do not need an excuse.

Midnight is soon ...

Midnight is soon, dreams are quietly melting.
There is an orange peel smell.
Someone's tears have frozen on the glass
Gleaming like black pearls behind a curtain.
This century is going away: a new century will begin.
This verge will court the sound of crystal.

* * *

Windows overlook all eyes,
Lanes stretche like a question.
Loving watches do not go back.
Your songs are popular.
Yet, you've forgotten the way to that land.
The changeable old harpsichord,
You are like the Milky moon, please play at night.
A minuet from the past meeting new constellations.
In misted windows, there is a shadow
Excitedly crying, remembering.
While lilac is heeling in magnificent blossoms,
These are thunderstorms of ravishing May,
A restrained gust of purple cherries,
The heat of arms burning hot like a wire.
They begged for a spare ticket at the box office,
It is a modest occasion for privacy.
But, the wind of wanderings will again bring
Old romances in the lane.
Where the lilac still blooms,
They believe in good-natured patience.
There are darkened windows' bright eyes.
Chrysanthemums are getting cold in the Czech vase -
There is a pattern of genuine affection.

14.12.2008

Raushan Burkitbayeva-Nukenova

Land of ancestors

I'm short of breath in a city apartment,
In the pompous, lined, underground.
My soul is in fate's hands – like a target in a shooting gallery.
A brutal cough exhausted my gut.

Peals of thunder like the volleys of a victory are
Flowing from the mountains beyond the horizon.
Washing away soot, fears, troubles, with the rain.
My umbrella will flares up like a parachute of hope.

I will leave the bustling city following this storm,
There are red fields of gentle poppies
And cornflowers' making shy eyes!
I will be warmed and healed by Mother Earth!

A sacred spring is in the marble baptistery.
There is a flock of playful, naughty, marinkas.
Juniper is along the banks. We both sit down,
Admiring our homeland.

Annual rings are closed circuits
The stubborn moon is flying through them.
Our mountains, steppes, are blessed.
A magic string of the dombra is ringing!

May 2009, Karatau

In Taraz

Tree crowns merge like arches.
I am going to school along Pushkin street.
All roads like memory lead to the bazaar
after years of separation in a misty delirium.

And here is the intersection of Pushkin and Gorky.
The familiar stand-pipe's skeleton is sticking out
like a spyglass on my vigilant past,
although bitter with inevitable tears.

Houses have gone, where my preschool years raced
by like a May thunderstorm.
And clear waters were up to the waist,
Where are the yards dear to my heart and eyes?

My nanny and mother, brother and friends all
they've gone...
But in the school there is still a joyful buzz.
And a smell of white acacias is near the house.
Grandmother's chair still creaks beneath my niece.

How magnificent peonies, irises flourish.
And again a school graduation ball will fade away.

Raushan Burkitbayeva-Nukenova

To Klara K

Yet another day
And the sorrow is deeper
That separates us by a wall.
Harsh February
Sighs silently
Yet, it smells with spring everywhere.

And the night that has stolen
Your smile,
Will not brighten heavens tent.
Cold hands are
Twitching a string,
But, forgotten fire will expire.

I will hear
A darling voice in the distance,
Having forgotten myself in a joyless dream.
But your sparkling laughter
Has been taken away by snows that melt outside.

Snow again caresses
The drooping lantern
Trying to turn it.
Cold January
Separating us forever
How can I live without my beloved?

The Wormwood Wind

The dawn is nearer,
The garden is waking up.
Our house is full of children's ploys.
And my granddaughter's
Familiar gaze is
Meeting old friends.

2011

To my father

My wise Father! My Father!
You are bedridden ...
With your easy and fast trot
You entrained everybody after you.
Without fear, we stubbornly flew to our goal,
Like a quiver sharpened as a well-aimed arrow.
You opened the world and expanded the boundaries,
Your bright-eyed looked about you.
Yet, strict and more significant than words,
Time proved ruthless.
But, everyone
Has to say goodbye to childhood,
To wake up from dreams.
And children pick their way forward.
Here grandchildren are chirping in their father's nest.
Comparing actions by strict evaluation,
We felt his gaze everywhere.
And if fate sent us troubles,
Father's heart was like a steel wall,
He shielded, supported, us to victory.
And we needed his smile more than medicine.
You are not broken by diseases, losses,
You walked proudly on glass.
Having harvested grains of wisdom,
Generously shared by serving them up.
The last example before becoming a legend
You taught us, bravely, to withstanding time.

The Wormwood Wind

Indeed, remembering your force,
we continued conversation.
Of a Father finishing life lessons!
Pumpkins, carrots, are grow in beds
And apple trees are heavily bowed with fruit.

July 27, 2013

Raushan Burkitbayeva-Nukenova

Railway station

From the darkness of snow
To wanderings around the world
The express train flew
In a symphony of sleepers.
Yet, having snoozed,
And always ready to give answers,
A sleepless station awaits meditating.

Accustomed to the hustle and separations,
To the whistles and sobs of express trains.
Through a desert of looks, distances,
Blown through by cold meetings.

It catches dropped stories.
There platforms are breathing thick air.
Yet, paints still lives and portraits
Of flashing nature abounds from all sides.

Here's a ghost - a satellite from a mad century
But, on time, we emerge from the darkness.
While roaring rivers like a steel node
Are intertwined in wintry bags.

The station stands as a fortress on the road
Defending the approaches of ages.
It summarizes all calculations and results
Under the banners of legendary flags!

The Wormwood Wind

A lop-sided, shabby,
Awkward house near the road -
Seems to be firmly rooted,
Dashing together with its century off the rails.

Raushan Burkitbayeva-Nukenova

At the railway station

A station stands like a giant.
Deaf from cries, sobs, sighs.
Here like fair showcases,
An era rushes madly!

Actors and extras are yelling,
Shuffling bags, drinking vodka.
Someone discusses a hunger strike
And waits for an exchange rate change.

In pursuit of a capricious lady
Everyone is fussing and racketing,
And behind the dusty window frame
Sad poles are gazing.

Like stuffing, and splashed with
Sweat, pushy people creep
Through already crowded doors,
Pulling bags and worries.
While toots are desperately sounding.

And now, wagons are cracking
And shelves groan from unnecessary weights,
And somewhere out there, beyond the haul,
Dim lights twinkle.

The Wormwood Wind

Here stands the station. And a waiting
Mother, anxious for many years,
Looks and looks again
At quiet windows.

Raushan Burkitbayeva-Nukenova

Railway station 3

The lamp grieves in vapours of fuel oil.
The barrier-cricket with a chilled trill
Hastens to comfort the blown-off bridge,
Telegraphing to April.

The platform decorated with petunias
Meets train compartments with music.
While trembling under these prattlers -
The station-father is at a zenith of fame!

The foremen are in uniforms,
The trainmen are waving their flags.
Tides of sudden feelings and repressed tears
Carry passengers far away.

Someone parts, someone meets!
There are waves of invading emotions.
New acquaintances - over a glass of tea.
- Please, Eskimo pie, four servings for us!

And over road networks -
There is a bridge, as if in eternal swoon.
But, this station is chilled from drafts
Deafened by a roll-call of counters.

Galloping century, the changes
Scare provincial cities.
Snows, rains - a lesson in patience.
The station is meeting an express train.

Cosmodrome

Baikonyr cosmodrome. Rockets.
Achievements of minds – like minarets
Rise above the poor landscape.
Behind the Ural in an aul, the debris
Of the carrier will explode.
Striking a match in the darkness - it will disappear.
Going up, step after step, into an abyss.
"Do you remember who the first was? -
Yuri Gagarin!
"Ah Kazakh Dzhigit? -
Tokhtar - our guy! "
But a radars' sensitive ears
Do not hear again - this underground roar.
From a bottomless space well.
The stars blankly look down,
They are not disturbed by terrestrial problems.
We are being explored by other worlds!
Vanity is not accepted,
By the silent, dignified desert.
Steppe-dwellers shall never leave their lands.
The old camel is proudly
Grazing at open spaces.
Aruana, darting off,
Rushes to its native land.
The livestock is healthy, let the offspring
Grow.
In dusty hats

Cities are sweating - acting high and mighty.
I pray for the aul.
Let water be transparent there!
The rest, I hope, will be added.

A mannequin and an ant

In the shop window, a plastic mannequin has stiffened
in new clothes from Gucci, Dior and Chanel - counting
people passing by with an impassive gaze.
It is bored - bed does not attract it.
Fearlessly, without pain, like a fir tree it sparkles
invitingly with lights.
Yet, it is fashion's willy-nilly hostage.
Enthusiasm and girlish dreams are not about it.
It never goes up on the podium.
Dior shines with the music made by lines.
However, the route of clouds is reflected in water.
Through the mirror-like surfaces of crazy lakes.
High standards dictate prices to all.
Masterpieces from tailors are pacing the stage.
Chests-of-drawers are cracking: wardrobes are spreading,
Eyes and classy diamonds are shining.
Flying off the carousel of endless things.
Our mannequin is hu-ma-ni-zed!
But, a box for bijouteries is bottomless.
And the whole world has lost colorful marbles.
It demonstrates to its showcase.
The core, however, peeps like a gray mouse.
While the soul crys silently, like the rain.
Who will feel a shiver of time?
Here an ant, after reviewing all the insides,
Is sighing bitterly – just junk afterall!
There is nothing for it to feast in here,

Raushan Burkitbayeva-Nukenova

Will anything be useful for its home?
And having been caught, it silently drags a paillette
Before hhastily leaving the glass cage.
But mannequin is indifferent to the ant.
Being so small, it has its own life!

***

Autumn, you have come to me uncalled,
Dropped like a yellow envelope in the window.
And peas of crimson rowanberries are
Bittering with the sorrow of days long gone.
Flocks of cranes are carrying this summer
Far away - and dawn meets with a chill.
Yet, dreams are still warmed by tenderness.
- Don't hurry, winter - some are screaming.
There will still be warm days.
And these nights will break out in a fire of passion,
And flying wedges like the lines of a song
Floating solemnly into the heaven
Reach autumn - which timidly knocls on the door,
Having taken off a wet cloak – go then, meet!
Cold banks are hidden behind the mist,
Let's sit down and have a cup of sweet tea.

***

When you go away - autumn comes to me.
And rain knocks on my window all night.
"What are you sad about?" - my girlfriends ask me.
Spring will come and everything will revive!

***

Here is August - it's a time of stargazing.
I'm flying in a chariot of desires.
Sparks go down, flashing somewhere near,
Seeing their light disappear with a sweet look
I want to make a wish.

Raushan Burkitbayeva-Nukenova

To Ravil and Lyubov

Again it is September. The moon is disappearing.
A sad garden is full of heavy fruits.
We are glad to the favored weather.
But, a ghostly earth cold is wandering.

I am carried like a squirrel into a hole
This whole hill of red apples -
A gift from friends and sunny days!
From the heights of years,
 I know better about friendship.

Autumn comes to life unnoticed.
My temple silvers with sadness,
Noting signs with paint,
Shadows of the past obliquely appeat.

Extending all-night vigils, the garden will
Guard my sensitive dream: waiting for spring
Blossom on apple trees, never blaming anyone!

22.09.2014

Talgar

***

How long a sleepless night is...
And let the growing moon,
That visits us,
Promise the joy of meeting.

261

Incredibly white night

Night is slipping like a stocking from the hip,
Exposing a strip of dawn.
A girlfriend is sleeping scantily clad.
And it's time for me to get back.
At home my mom holds an age long question:
"Tell me, where the hell you have been?"
"And when will you become serious!"
 Yet, the entrance door shakes because of wind.
Sleeping, sleeping, till getting blue in the face.
A hated alarm clock rings.
How can I justify another delay?
"Once again, you'll be fired!"
Days shift nights in duck-legged motions.
Faces of old and new friends.
Never changing us for the better.
Debt holes make me feel heavy-hearted.
Passengers experiencing sleepless nights
Run about like angry breezes,
Through the mist, like spilled pop wine,
Leaving a bunch of keys.
Life is a pitcher broken by others -
Set tos, ins and outs ...
A myth is forgotten like a cave stone
In a shaky building of persistent times.
- You have chosen a ridiculously wrong way   -
And will be ruthlessly swept away -
The diagnosis of doctors is merciless.

Raushan Burkitbayeva-Nukenova

Take a breath! And look again at the sky -
Every day there are boiling clouds.
Demand honesty from your heart.
Following centuries of indulgent tales.
While hope semaphores its blinking.
The Neva has not becoming warm over the years.
Naked Venus in the Summer Park hardly excites a
teenager.
(Tatars are guilty in everything!)
Bridges will be raised again regretting
The separation of a long night.
Virgins are freezing in the apartments, in the alleys
And a sleepless daughter gets pale.
A ghost city on the waves of Fontanka
Joined together for centuries.
It remembers the song of a sad fugitive,
The one that this river extolled excitedly.

09.12.2014

***

Close to each other,
We make our way blindly.
And the rain, like a friend,
Is glad to our reconciliation.
In a busy Café
Umbrellas dry, being lined up in a row.

***

The Moon is a helpmate to love,
Illuminating a path for lovers.
And he, inspired by the moon,
Is again making his way to me
Through all encumbrances under the sun!

Kings of Pop and Rock and Roll

You are sitting in the dark – yet, a grate is on the window.
Frozen like a birder - hoping to strike.
A spider is crawling – dragging its shadow along the wall,
Weaving a frame - for the captured word.
Here's something to hold the spirit - "Wow, cool!"
It underlaid sideswiping,
I hold my breath- but it floods out of my throat,
Pushing my senses away - into the bloodstream!
I am focusing on hot shots,
Diluting them with strong alcohol.
In the same way a stadium hungers for hits - balls,
A multitudinous roar flies over the field.
And the more impudent – the more flammable the fuse is.
Through torn jeans – as verse material
I grow in every nerve and flesh of
Consonants - being an epitome of sin.
And even the diva Montserrat
Agreed to praise the stage-
In a duet that would have conquered a hit parade.
So small are the stars that fly to take their place.

12.12.2014

The Wormwood Wind

Raushan Burkitbayeva-Nukenova

Chapter 8

Star - sagebrush

Knowledge is power!

To Professor Stephen Hawking

Scaling yourself against the abyss of space,
Gliding along the edge of this black abyss
Of unprecedented troubles,
Your Physics – so clear and complex
Radiates the light of knowledge in our world.
As a great thing glimmers in the small heart.
Encased in a singularity disease.
Yet, you serve as an ideal for students,
And all your books have become popular.
A mighty spirit through a jungle of hidden spots.
Like the quantum of energy – you are a citizen
of the Universe!
The flight is amusing, the thoughts are immense,
You're preparing your a big blast again!

***

*There could be whole antiworlds and antipeople made out of
antiparticles. However, if you meet your antiself, don't shake
hands! You would both vanish in a great flash of light."
A Brief History of Time. Stephen Hawking*

I know that meeting is —
        The beginning of separation..
And the heart is like a compass
        For lost woman,
Who protracts fire
        But the numb handed.
Poets are wedded forever
        To the Muse.
Where is that depth
        That is bottomless like space?
Feelings, like the poison of acid rains
        Are superficial.
The sadness of the Sistine Madonna
        Is inescapable
The Vatican keeps its bullae
        In papal leaders.
Centuries have passed already,
        But ink does not dry.
And the fragile peace of a dream
        Will violate confusion.
And what about the upper classes,
        Are they still deaf?
Or, again, will purification be
        Hurled like a flood?
In a farewell letter
        The river is sealed.
But the sun will crush ice,
        And rip off wax.

Step into space -
                There is a long-awaited meeting,
In an abyss of galaxies -
                Behind the nebula of clouds!
Herds of clouds are
                Blown by the wind -shepherd,
A scientist in the night
                Strains his ears.
And black holes
                Keep all the secrets.
They are also stars
                Born of cold winds.
And for science there are no limits,
                Prohibitions.
An extraterrestrial
                Meets comets.
The indestructible spirit is
                Ready to exploit!

Raushan Burkitbayeva-Nukenova

Silence of the moon

The flower that stretches to glamorous heaven
Is nature beautious in its own unkowing.
And the cloud that flies past,
Groans with longings inexplicable.
Also, rain fallen from unimaginable heights
Will revive once in unkowable symphony.
When in the depth of disturbed ponds.
Yet, who knows the secret of dying gardens.
Since, each time, burnt by love,
The enamored crescent soars like a boomerang.
And interrupting each other waves
In gossip pointless, silence is best offered
to the moon.
And dew, like the tears of a pale diva -
Motivates the anticipated of seperation.
While attentive stars blink
And melt silently in the gloomy distance.

***

You have grasped the mystery of magic -
Captured a beautiful moment
And now it lasts for centuries.
And your hand remembering this gesture.
Allows our blood to be excited by
A love thought long extinct!

***

Like two ends,
Right and left,
We cannot keep promises.
Forever linked, instead, by the belt of desire,
Unable to escape from each other.

Star – wormwood

In the window – there is only a bitter
Starlight of hopes shot dead.
They do not wait for... steps taken in a dark thicket -
Where a deceptive moon makes no oval.

Heavy snow, it is overwhelming,
Like an awareness of disaster.
But in dark night-times the park dreams
About alleys and the smell of mignonette.

On the dance floor in a blameful manner,
Having leant that lights are waiting for you.
The snowstorm, hugged by insomnia,
Plays orchestral melodies until dawn.

Only on paper peacefully
In memories come to life, those,
Whom you loved so dearly,

Raushan Burkitbayeva-Nukenova

Are poisoned in a pond by beach wormwood.

And your heart has gone blind without her,
The world has fallen into a void.
And colours are burned to ash,
As death has won beauty.

The play is over, and the stage
Keeps its magic of love.
The actor has gone away ...
And there is no substitution,
Do not wait in vain. Do not call.

And only happy faces,
And your tender youth are in the pictures.
You will see your sweetheart in your dreams.

And to the last breath,
As long as you live – She is with you!
Yet, pain does not stop in your chest.

March 2014

***

The day burns down like a candle.
And faded leaves replace the gloss.
When light diminishes in the eyes -
The dance of earth hours is interrupted.
And turning to dust, sand,
I want to stay in my native land.
Where the high sky ceiling will
Touch my face with snowflakes
Petals of crunchy pages will
Reveal secrets in a new light.
Like a gleaming thoughtful river,
I will flicker for a moment in my grandchildrens,
children.
Yey, years of accumulated grievances
Hide stones in their silence.
Let everyone forgive themselves!
Otherwise, cargo will turn into weightless dust.
Healing streams flow
Through clay, marble blocks.
Wormwood bitters like a parting,
Although, coastal curves attract.
When the day fades away on the steppe,
Night ensnares.
Cheer up, wait for the dawn.
Spring will meet you with tulips!

28.11.2012

Defile

And outside the night defiles
As instants disappear in a star wilderness.
Someone's fate and someone's vision
Will flash in a smile and hide away
From the ice-hole of dim mirrors.
Suddenly a distinct profile emerges.
I looked for you, my forgotten friend,
Why should we pay off old scores?
In rustling keys – there are gusts of sadness,
Hidden music, a trembling of time.
The rain, slaving away, creates motives
Like an unexpected revelation.
There are rusty spots where gilding -
On the wet foliage of shiny roofs one occured.
Autumn with its thinning brush
Will leave canvases as a keepsake
But, will not hear ...

02.09.2014

Melancholy

You are not in a millionaires city
It is empty.
There are no leaves underfoot -
There is only a crisp first snow.

You have left for Lisbon -
As silky night's bite
Into the sweetest sound in this world -
The sound of your keys!

The ancient city

To Karl Baypakov

Millennium town is -
        In the labyrinth of the night.
Amu Darya has run away ...
        There is a stuffy captivity along our roads.
The snake is rattling, having split -
        A gestured death sting.
Like a wizened old man,
        The firm saksaul is chilled.
And time, like sand,
        Slips through your fingers.
And stars splash in the sky,
        Whisking strange milky juices.
Peals of dusty storms are -
        Like the rain of civilizations!
The day does not hear threats
        Aimed at the temple.
The potter circle of the sun
        Is red hot from the heat,
Screwed up, it sculpts again
        Apitcher, a tandoor side.
But the enemy is griping a bow,
        And arrows are eager to fight.
There will come a time for a battle,
        When blood will flow into the stream.

The Wormwood Wind

The hot wind will scuttle
>The remains of an old life.
And the beam shines timidly
>As if scared by the moon.
In the adobe bricks -
>Findings are like a surprise,
Through the dust and soot of clouds!
>Shine eyes - like a string of beads,
In blades – there are eyebrows,
>Only visible to a finder.
Kobyz sings about grief,
>But, ash is still warm.
It heals a snake's bite!
>Gurza crawled into the hole.
Smells of wine
>Have not yet escaped the jar!
It soaked the walls,
>And pokes into the nose
Awaken memories within me,
>Maybe because of this
Like a kui – of a familiar star,
>The dunes are singing
In the sands of Altyn-Emel about
>The bitterness of wormwood,
Passed caravans.
>Laid down dzhusan in the darkness.
Like an unwound turban
>There flows a silky rivulet.

Raushan Burkitbayeva-Nukenova

It was once married
        To the sea by a wave.
The Dombra sings about it
        And birds echoe the song
With the two-horned Alexander
        Behind a rampart!
The steppe keeps its sullenly silence
        From the pain of old wounds.
Balasagun, Otrar, Taraz, Sairam, Sauran
        Shed, Iasi, Sygnak, Merke, Kulan ...
The road winds
        Like a silk scarf.
The archaeologist's look is -
        Strictly investigative.
Terracotta glitters
        With an interwoven openwork ornament!
The scientists' work is
        Painstakingly meticulous.

Asia

Steppe vastnesses
With no end in sight
Delights the eye,
Blooming in the spring.
A green moire of
Silk grasses,
Encouraged praises for the steppe by
Abai and Mukhtar!

Traditions, customs
Are unchanged there.
Climate, nature
Give their law.
Asia fell into
Stupor.
Contemplation -
Is its being.

Soaked asphalt,
Shines with anthracite,
Roads fade away
Beyond the horizon.
A firing range is closed,
The nuclear umbrella scaled down!

Away from the Giants
Of civilization

Raushan Burkitbayeva-Nukenova

Rest and peace receive an ovation here!
Fate prepares
A lonely spot,
In the desert
As rivers' mouths end.

Amid the sky
A missile path fades,
Piercing like a needle
Into the cloudiness of years.
Let the heart of
The steppe mainland
Fill with light
These age long days!
And let the river-memory
Feed earth

Tragedy of Aral

There, high up in the sky
Circling, an eagle hovers while a merlin is after it.
Have you heard that vultures behind seven seals
Hide secrets?
Seagulls like mournful messengers melt.
Wise people assure us,
Time will heal the pain of loss.
The Aral Sea dries up,
An old fisherman takes apart his net.
Barges are in salty, rusty burns.
Takyrs like psoriasis scabs
Fly over the roofs and carpets.
There is an asylum of leprosy
It is hot and a fierce wind blows.
Water disappears - as life and people follow it.
The symposium, the debates are like beating air,
Amudarya and Syrdarya
Flowed to the Aral – in braids.
Channels unbraided those rivers -
In poisoned stripes.
Greed and blindness ruin nature.
Korkyt Ata cannot find peace!
Kobyz cries of distress, it may awaken the world.
Outlines of the state borders -
Destroy the sea of indifference,
Gathering tears of rice
In a rich harvest.

Raushan Burkitbayeva-Nukenova

The Great Silk Road
Stretched in a wave of caravans.
The ships - from the Caspian Sea to the Aral Sea,
In an affluent continuous string,
About which the song's dragging sadness refrians.
Mangyshlak, like weathered reefs
Is where eagles chase foxes.
Aytyskers hunt after successful rhymes.
And oil is like caked blood on someone deceased,
Who furiously fought and loved.

***

A genetic memory lives in each of us ,
not felt in everyday life, but sometimes
flashing in the subconscious.
                        L. N. Gumilev

Where does fate carry you?
What does the shaman tell us?
Here the Ulba runs to the Irtysh,
And the Milky Way shows the route.
How fragile is our glass world
There is nothing tighter than a mammoths flesh.
And our ecumenical feast is brief
Since somewhere invisible Fate wanders.

***

One remembers in bad weather
July thunderstorms' hammering rain,
And violent nature,
And this shivering virgin.
When a hail of memories
Suddenly shooting the heart dead,
You shall recover from the subconscious
As heights flying into the deep,
Below which there still
Rushes a rapid river.
Where a generous hand gifted
So much joy and tenderness.

Raushan Burkitbayeva-Nukenova

Guard

Night suddenly has hidden
In mysterious decoration,
And in nomadic space -
There is a knock.
On its creaky arba
The fat moon sweeps around with a bored look
Into sleeping houses.
It watches once again sufferings and passions.
Shining in silence with a quiet sadness
Like a lantern.
While in the morning - having got tired to death,
It finds nothing to cry about.
It will entrust the sun undividedly
To intersection our dreams.

***

I'm jealous of the sun,
It caresses you,
Warming you despite the wind
On this September day.
I envy the shadow
That's in its hurry for you,
Merged with am image of the night
To find peace.
I wish I were the air.
Then without me
You could not live
A minute, a day.

Raushan Burkitbayeva-Nukenova

Mystery of night

What does the stream sing about to the shadow?
Or the shade of the thick elms ...
What does the cicada chirp about in the garden?
And to whom does the lamp give its light?
Throughout the day and night
What does the wave sing about to the wave?
From the hypnotic trance,
In complex solitaire hands,
I am trying to see by chance,
What a mystery means.
And in ritual dances through the night
Chase boredom and fear away.
But the stars are so nice,
Because they are not available to the soul.
And through the glass of a fragile universe
They give us a smiling light.

The Moon

Unpretentious and simple like an aster,
Growing in a flowerbed near the club -
The moon rose like a flower made of alabaster
And becomes a symbol sung by a cube.
Epithets, comparisons, enthusiasm
Are sent to it by poets as flowers thrown on a stage.
Although, never trading, they will cease,
It was and will be a priceless lady!
Admirers in swarms are
Around it – an unfading lamp.
At the disco as night music plays,
The stars groove in a lambada with it.

In the worlds of love – of unfaithful comet -
The way of proved orbits is closed for us!
The earth will not destroy the reality of our dreams -
Lights of the midnight suns beckon us.
Those who dream and remember the names-
They are not given the joy of meeting in their love ,
But dark raptures of parting!
M. Voloshin

Raushan Burkitbayeva-Nukenova

Where did batyrs go?

Where did batyrs go?
Nobody raised a sword!
Yet, the sounds of the lyre will go silent -
Without his praise.
Men are different today;
Pompous, stupid
They do not notice a soul
And are blind like moles.
Obedient to wind, power.
Bending their backs as feather grasses,
And where are the old passions -
Horsetail have dragged in the dust for a long time.
And where is steppe pride?
Where is a high-spirited argamak?
Decisiveness and firmness,
A painstaking fist?
Steppe athletes are
Steeped in legends...
But you are mocked by wives.
Is there a force, which can whip?

Fountain of love, fountain alive!
As gift to I've brought two roses
I love your unceasing talk
And poetic tears
A.S. Pushkin

Great Silk Way

The ancient roads are forgotten,
And caravans are not visible anymore,
And there is no trace of former alarms.
Only ruined towers.
All noise died down. Getting stuck in mud.
Stubborn donkeys looked for a yard.
When the sound of silver was ringing in a jar
So stunned, the vastness stood motionless.
But, now there is no life behind those dusty walls,
Though bricks endure.
Messengers are not seen on the roads,
The whistle of a tight whip no longer heard.
Age old lamps keep heat,
While the ligature of sky-blue bowls does not fade.
Yet, only the voice of steppe beliefs
Maintain these links with our past!

Raushan Burkitbayeva-Nukenova

The pain of Genghis Khan

The night is poisoned by bitter wormwood
And dark thoughts like herds of
Mad horses that wheeze over the desert
Shake all dreams by a worse nightmare.
And a slave hides in fear in the corner,
Alas, he does not need her caresses.

The Universe Shaker is severe and gloomy.
Sometimes his furious eyes are mad.
He cannot forgive an unwitting betrayal
And washes his agonizing, bitter, shame.

Like a fierce wind, he rushes over the steppe.
He wants to forget his burning pain,
But, rumors abound that an iron chain
Ruined love with its grin.

On the steppe, a smoky fire dies,
It smells of hot and dusty sagebrush,
And stars. like captives, enter his tent,
While slaves groan with pain, shyly.

A pitcher from the tool shed

A pitcher was found
By Imangali Tasmagambetov
in 1996.

In the empty pitcher
   Lives a booming wind
And at night it sings
   Painfully over the steppe .
And its sobs
   Do not let me fall asleep,
It looks for the lost
   Silk Road.
In a silver bell
   Let the stars lead.
Seekers will find
   Coins in the house.
And refill
   It to the edges,
And it will find
   Its lost roof.
The pitcher grieves and
   Dries up from melancholy.
For a long time it has not seen
   An emerald river,
Where the waters of Zhaik
   Caressed it springily
In the fragile neck
   There shone the moon.

But in the dust of ages
          Memories languishe despondently;
- Can it be true that the hostess
          Has forgotten me?
In silence there is no sound of
          The ring jingle,
Beats of excited
          Young hearts.
When she pressed it
          To her bossom like a hope,
The pitcher trembled
          In her arms.
- From the distance of ages
          Like a blue bird -
I believe – life will again
          Be reborn in the desert,
Fill me
          With running water.
And a chimney will flare up
          Over the asleepy river ...

Hadj

A short summer melted like frost.
Sisters wore out blue cotton dresses.
Cities, countries, drifted in fog like a mirage,
Like a shaky vision in the desert -
Like a caravan sailing into history
On the rustling sand – in the singing dunes
Someone's song is covered by a whirlwind
on the mound.
In the thrall of time, in the deep zindan.
Like the red mane of a bareback mare -
There is a tail from a burning comet-fugitive.
Hands in a prayer to heaven are uplifted,
Grandfather sees signs in a fiery dance.
Myths weave their stories.
Great-grandfather goes to Mecca to the sunset
in crimson.
Songs of Bedouins' lutes are plaintive.
An inflamed brain from the heat of midday
Dreams of cool rain.
The guide of an Arab leader sings.
On the horizon there emerges a mirage.
Like a target, there is a gazelle in the peephole
of carbines.
They aims at it "Hey, Abdullah do not miss!"
Tears of a pounded victim – in stinging
Drops of rain from the desert ...
And grandfather continues his way to Medina,

Praying - finishes his Hadj.
Now it is much easier -
Flying through Sharjah,
Then by a fleet of buses.

Grandmother's Bracelets

The matt gloss of our showcase mirrors ...
For a long time, you have diligently sough such trails.
Your bracelets jingling like a song.
From oblivions shadows, where it is depressing
and cramped.
Like the light of goodness itself - gentle handed,
Your grandson carefully carried your bracelets.

- When tired of vacabularies heat
You'll want pleasant dreams -
I'll be like a shade at the road,
My swift-footed colt.
You are an invaluable light of my eyes
You performed my prophetic covenant.
And the singing of times gone
Sounds aloud from all sides!

Parting

The chest of the yurt keeps heat in the night,
But parting winfs cry like a cuckoo.
A heavy quiver is full of gloomy dreams.
Stay with me I'm begging you: otherwise
I'll burst into tears.

Why my dear, you need midday light,
When I am not next to you in the saddle.
And we truly need to be happy,
And this chance is given only once ...

The dawn burns out with lips of flame,
And tired stars quenched the morning light.
And again, parting cries like a cuckoo
And again my heart aches with pain.

Raushan Burkitbayeva-Nukenova

Starling-houses

Starling-houses are seldom in cities,
Where pavements are covered with asphalt.
I remember the blossom of cherry trees,
That showered the boulevard with flowers.
In spring, I together with my brother, tried
To hammer together a palace from planks
And climbed rickety stairs,
Waited: where was our new tenant?
He flew with an unearthly song,
One acquired during its travels.
The cherry trees stood motionless - embarrassed ,
While enchanted jasmine bloomed .
And we looked at the emerald world
Through glass broken by someone.
And it seemed to us it was easy to fly,
To see the village beyond the river.
Well, now we have taken off from the land
Like birds.
The eye pits of houses looking into distances,
Althoug, they have grown dim because of cold winter.
But as soon as the air smells of spring,
Crows will fly away like a nightmare.
Under the window, we, my son,
Will erect a house for these songstresses!

Native home

Grass faded. Fences became shabby
The sun reigning fdown on a shabby house.
Frost draws patterns on the windows,
Our village stands motionless in languishing slumber.

The cuckoo cuckooed for dinner,
Sweets in the vase lay as an untouched hill.
Summer passes, but guests do not come,
Frost covers our porch with a thick crust.

Nights are longer, walks are shorter,
We drink thyme tea with raspberry.
Everybody, finally, got together in the alley,
My fathers jacket has absorbed the smell of sweat.

Speeds and distance have grown up
I have no time, but my parents are waiting.
Do not extend the period of separation,
Apples are freezing in the Garden of Eden.

Raushan Burkitbayeva-Nukenova

Broken dishes -Mean good luck!
Do not cry, the beauty ...
Yuri Entin

Kachalova, Michurina-
These are two streets from childhood.
My memory is looped in them
With friends in the neighborhood.
Noisy crowds
Coming together in for games.
Above dusty ravines
Long evenings have melted
Like years in a smoky room.
Racing railway cars around the world.
Only a squinting glance from the sun
With unrequited love
We are kissed by the wind,
Awakened by anxieties.
Our thoughts as lace,
Above knitting needles from overworked times.
Through the creaking of an loaded cart,
Grunts of glass bottles are heard.
We hear the cry affected by cold:
"Where are you, old coachman?"
Utensils - "U-tensils!" -
In exchange for a coin sound.
Tell me, where our neighbours
Quitely went?

The Wormwood Wind

And the windows nodded.
With a blind moon
We are reflected in glasses
In a wandering crowd.
Yet our song will be interrupted,
Akthough, upraised like a flag!
But, it will respond to invocations.
By the clicks of latches!

10.09.2014

Imangli

Enveloping with a look like felt,
Your warmth protecting us from cold and envy.
Awfule goodies are made to rejoice.
And cannot be dragged from temptation

It detonates everything it touches!
And then, scatters like a rumour.
Shining like a day above the capital,
You will come into girls' dream many times.

You are the reason for hopeless longing
And you cannot escape from yourself.
Drink your morning capu-chi(n)o
Served by a secretary - marriage wrecker!

The Wormwood Wind

***

A pit is caved in the sky
Where I stumbled on your story.
All day, I wandered in clouds of fog
And inspiration has not come.

In Paris, the sky turns pink,
In Milan, they celebrate a show.
The north sobers due to wind,
Refuse will hit with coldness.

Empty eye sockets are sad,
September reflects in them,
A chill from our aging capital,
Braiding the meshes of October.

When, with finest cobwebs
The last heat is caught,
With our plot inserted into pictures,
Rain will precipitate in the village!

27.09.2014

Raushan Burkitbayeva-Nukenova

***

The garden embarrassed by the attention of
Passersby, flushes with a bow of branches.
The greedy eyes of the townspeople do not worry,
This garden keeps its dignity in silence.

It beckons us deep into elated flesh - saturating
As thunderstorms saturate chords.
Bunches of apples are clustered tightly -
Bounty is disappearing from country gardens!

The garden looks tired, strictly -
Although, it feels a little sorry for us.
We are bucking along dusty roads,
And in the mountains - even herbs are fresh!

The city breathes like an old asthmatic
Grumbling because of a growing jam.
While rain saturated with corroding acid
Nearly washes the shamed roof away.

The aroma of these apples in the apartment,
Will leak to the staircase,
Eclipsing other recipes in the air.
We will eat them with pleasure!

Like the crimson cheeks of rural women
Who keep the heat of their kisses!

The Wormwood Wind

We're going out of town bright and early,
Riding, showing off, and prancing!

So ridiculous are our clothes out there.
We all seem like fashionable kids.
Flying over the precipice ... and the lash
We dissect the mist with laughter!

The garden has taken a space in our heart,
After renovation, it awaits us each season.
The garden is an inventor instead of constancy
It takes us to the mountains beyond the horizon!

I pray my friends – Save
This dear garden - abode.
Knowing this grim century is a destroyer.
The garden agrees with me - Love !!!

24.09.2014

Raushan Burkitbayeva-Nukenova

***

The April square thrilled with warm weather.
There's a flock of white butterflies -
Medical students from now on,
The hostages of Latin,
Are caught in lingering fetters.

Spring! A luxury lilac causing
My head to go round,
Without an approving zeal
To boring cramming and humility,
Haven forgotten all rules and words.

A college girl is flying through the years
Like a winged butterfly. And in the window -
There's a lilac bush hugged by sadness,
It is whispering something at my heels
Like a guilty admirer.

And in the park a flock of songbirds twitter - thrilling
with warm weather.
But the astringent taste of wormwood
Bitters, and the frost glistens like silver
And there are no familiar faces around me...

04.02.2014

In the Port

The outgoing evening
Was looking for swift passing meetings,
Like a rakish drunk wind,
Bypassing the river station.
It gazed at faces
And got up on its toes.
Caughting a smile,
At the bored oval.
And dashing shadows of
Runaway hours were
Short of breath with excitement,
The bolt bar was aching deceitfully.
And the floorboards were creaking
In the stuffy cabin of the night.
Party girls were waiting,
A commonplace hit sounded.
Clouds raced, getting drunk.
The Milky Way popped up in a river.
The Ghost Town turning to stone
Was cooling down in a forgetful dream of itself.

Raushan Burkitbayeva-Nukenova

***

It is the end of January and again, it snows heavily.
Belated desert words are that snowflakes still race each other.
As far as the nearest forest, the nearest river,
Snowdrifts whiten like high stacks,
I'm wandering in circles along a parkway
Hoping to grasp the wings
Of a hovering bird - what workmanship.
And it would be a mistake to judge me severely,
Every river paves the way to someone,
While, through rocks waterfalls have thundered for ages.
But, confused rains sounds at the wrong moment
And timid herbs start to make play.
Only dishevelled couples will awake in the morning.
Poetry is a suspension of enchanted dreams.
Although, critics will appreciate my strange harvest.

28.01.2014

***

Waiting for the first push - ad nauseam
I am eager for the away from airless lies.
After all, lines (like prisoners) have endurance,
Contrary to the fated murder of crows.
Who experience a flight filled with bliss,
And rush upwards, ringing with metaphors
To fill this world with an announced perfection
Becoming the music of the awakened day!

***

To Erkesh Shakeev

What do you add to this music?
Every day leaving to the sunset.
The black-and-white colours of the keys -
Intonations - sobbing of rain.
From the chords of a mountain summer
The sheet is marked with a hail of notes
Clouds are melting, and songs is not sung.
Yet, a look at the star abyss is radiant.
As cherries shake with transparency.
Juice is ravishing to the lips ...
With distant, unearthly tunes
A trumpet raves in booming echo.

20.06.2011

Chapter 9
Metamorphoses

***

A canopy thawed from bliss...
One day it rains, another day it hails,
and then it snows.
Yet, the mad flirting of stars takes too long,
So passionate is a frank look.
Oh, how tempting is the vastness,
So delightful are dreams!
Eyes beckon with aquamarine
So attractive are features.
While some stars are falling wearily
Into your open palm.
The Universe rings, sings in a small snowflake –
and you touch it!
In the metamorphosis of the day and night
Do not look for a brutal truth.
You will find a folded star map -
Through the bendings of melted peaks.

Raushan Burkitbayeva-Nukenova

***

The transparent fabric of heaven's longing
Is stitched with threads of rain.
And people starve for breath-in(stant)spirations,
Entering life and leaving.

In this maelstrom of love, an Alchemist
Will mix a list of names.
In the intertwining of fates, lines
The lunar disk is secretly involved.

The steppe mumbles under creaking carts.
Like a scar - an opening gapes through it.
Raided by straying clouds,
which burst into a thunderstorm.

Transforming this energy boost,
The blast creates an even greater one!
From dots of stars, elegies
A melody-gust is flying.

There someone ravels threads.
As the snow knits laces.
"Sketches", "Labyrinth" by Schnittke.
And Claude Mane paints "Haystacks"
Degas – ballerinas' flights!

26.11.2014

311

To Ainagul

It is still February, but the temptation is so great,
And empty caramels of ice are nasty.
Let's escape to the edge of a dream, on roofs without fear
To a country where amber and wild hop triumph.
A glassblower plays at inventing vases.
A chorus of icicles is hoarsened welcoming spring.
And sadness melts quietly, invisibly before our eyes,
Upcoming flowers will awake the pine.
Longings and dreams, and pain and joy, tears -
As one sip of wine matures in silence.
And March prepares for us tulips and mimosa.
Your sadness will settle to the bottom like a stone.
And even an extra day bestowed to us -
From on high - will not raise difficulties for us.
And now there glides like snow across wet roofs
A spring breeze of meetings appointed by destiny!

***

Like an apple tree in blossom, you graced the gray world.
You filled with spring my stuffy room.
How brief this moment is, I am sorry about this.
I passionately love you, my soul!

Raushan Burkitbayeva-Nukenova

The world behind the looking-glass

To Liza

The lake surface is powdered with snow,
Asleep leaves - through the thin crust of ice.
December is solemnly silent – as bliss seizes star
ceilinfs in a sleepy kingdom.
The lonely Moon is wandering like Ophelia.
The snow is streaming through the fog like powder.
And marvelous (far away) musical wanderings fill
a sleeping volcano like a cup.
Happiness languishes in mirrored fragments,
It cannot be cither collected or stuck together.
And past lives are gathring dust in museums,
Bold ideas will come to life in a drawing.
While the sun drinks wine from a papal warehouse
And beating waves breathe through the pines' music.
There are moving shadows at the mirror settings.
We are echoes: the cry of seagulls over black water.

***

My finger ring is
Squeezed by this ring.
There is a young bright face in the frame.
Happiness was close - I did not listen to it.
And the fading oval has merged
With anguish.

***

"Flowers smell sticky in the garden"
A magnificent evening is driving into the yard.
Where clouds are haughty riders.
Let them keep secret our conversation.
And rains, like hopes, before autumn, will
Mature and collapse along oir wall.
Saddened snow will fall in a streak of gray.
You, unfortunately, did not stay with me.
Our garden is clouded with a quiet sadness,
A star will prick someone's heart.
Yet, over the years these wounda will be healed,
Trains will lull us.
And the moon will flying like a ball,
Between the roofs of our houses.
Lilac blooms along the fence,
The evening is thrilled with spicy smokes.

02.02.2009

Raushan Burkitbayeva-Nukenova

***

In the arid desert,
On mountain ridges,
In the thawed tundra -
Glades are flowering.
And women are also
Like flowers:
A woman explodes there
Where she is loved and waited for!

***

Listen to the river, to its vivid funk.
Oh, sometimes it burns with a fever at night!
Under the wings of bridges,
in the embrace of winter blizzards -
There are trembling hoses in blockaded Leningrad.
That great river is the foremother of stanzas, symphonies,
A forehead, although our exhausted Neva swells with ice.
Shivering bows in whitened hands
Will throw out the sounds of spiers, sirens, blueness.
Fogs will float victoriously above the city.
And in the rivers mirror there is a familiar silhouette,
There nights will lighten,
while chestnuts accompany candlesticks
And waves will respectfully award the author with a bouquet.

***

The wind blows clouds away -
A pile of careless words,
And sadness gnaws our soul.
Who will help you in your trouble?
Relieve you from the caresses of that night?

Raushan Burkitbayeva-Nukenova

To K. Saltanat

A bench with a smell of paint

Is washed by sweet rain
Looking cautiously at a clock plate

We are hurrying on a date
And above jasmine hangs up

Like clouds of bees in a fleet
I am rescued from May storms.
By willow-shrub thick greenery
And lilac with a guilty smile.

Flowers burst like umbrellas.
A fountain, with greeny water,
Assaults ringing bridges.
Waxy chestnuts carry
Candles above these sidewalks.
Guards are on duty
And stars sing arias
My old park - a hermitage of love
You remember grannies and mummies
A holy guardian of family's legends
Flinging fragrance around us.

16.02.2009

***

My old house soaked to the skin,
Began squatting at the knee ...
By a lop-sided wicket gate
My mother was waiting for my father - off shift.
The moon pilaf was being stewed in the kazan,
The samovar was buzzing like bees.
Strings were waving with hanging linen.
And my brother was starting at a fire.
Our family was waiting beneath grapes,
Having laid a luxury dastarkhan.
And having examined everybody with a severe look,
He sat like a cruel Khan.
Puffy cakes were steaming.
Against plague squads of uninvited wasps.
And I turned cherries -' pair earrings
Into my outfit.
And my brother was suppressing
The fiendish onsurge of a green tomato.
My girlfriends were waiting outside the fence.
Yet, the world has forgotten such mirrors.

Raushan Burkitbayeva-Nukenova

***

My Taraz is like a blooming garden,
There - windows and doors are open to paradise -
Oh, you are a cradle of lovely peries!
I saw you just once.
(Oh, how carelessly you laughed!)
But, I've lost my peace forever.

***

In the arms of rain
I would wander into the park,
Sliding like a squirrel
On sleeping benches.
And take bunches of rowan
With me,
To make tincture for us
Based on songs-remakes.
"A hot hot-dog, Pepsi, icy Ice-Tea?" -
Are thrust them under our noses at the roadside cafe.
"Hot Grog, prepared jelly,
A handful of daisies in the needles of ice cream! "
I dry an umbrella of palm trees at the counter.
And the bartender looks incredulously, suspicious.
The mistress-leech has swelled out of spite -
He shows us the door into continued rains.
Lets get away with them: let's go dancing on the lawns.
Braiding the rainbow at dawn,
Breathing rosemary, lime, ozone,
Nibbling, munching at a cloud with apples!
The, having tired of tricks, we'll fall asleep
Where the night patiently mends its nets.
And the rain guards me under my window.
Breakfast, however, is cooked for us by adult children!

Raushan Burkitbayeva-Nukenova

Poet and idolatresses

Lifes semicircle is measured by
Tears, sweat, and steps.
And a faithful, old friend is near
Along with those whom we love.
And those whom I loved long ago,
Did not knock at my door.
I have changed my address, phone number.
My wife still believes me.
But what happened last spring,
Does not let me go - like a pain.
The Moon with its elastic bowstring
Of arrows, keeps a remembrance.
And April was in the yard,
And the sun was splashing in puddles.
Shaggy drunkenness wandering in blood,
You caressed shamelessly.
While quiet suburban cottages slept,
Where the poet – hermit lived,
Corks shot to the ceiling,
You canceled Monday.
And firewood popped into the stove,
And you read my poems.
As grass pierced through snow,
Yet, dawn was expelled from the hall.
Now twilight reigns,
Cold February is in my soul.
Don't follow youth, you fool.

The Wormwood Wind

A hungry cat sleeps by the oven.
I'll bake potatoes in the ash,
A steppe bird screams in the night.
But this candle does not extunguish,
And the page is not written ...

12.11.2008

Raushan Burkitbayeva-Nukenova

To B. Pasternak

"A frozen abscess of paved roads is scratched"-
Pasternak summarized one hundred years ago.
A century has flown, but in the same manner
The stubborn wind is fencing the sign with barriers.
"Hey, go around!" Here, they are dug into trenches,
Like de-miners are hurrying to help.
Machinery has come to a standstill.
"Go ahead, the diggers!"
This century's attempts will make the frost laugh.
Yet, you'll behold nature's maneuvers in this -
It is concerned by the smoke of clouds!
In the yards - instead of children's roars-
Cars are howling - raising their hips.
And a birch is growing stunted on the wayside,
It is time for it to use a gas mask.
A horse with a wagon has become a wonder.
The blizzard will present to us a "Khan's decree!"
The wind in the yard from the neighborhood
Has overtaken clouds, having curtained the window.
An ice crust is chilling the brake pads,
The city surrendered to winter's yoke long ago!
Someday everyone will strike the balance...
Due to a phantom poet.
Salt corrodes tires and roads.
Hard work is a preparation for winter.
The wind is a supporter of seasonal vagaries,
Sweeping into the yard in a star-like snowstorm.

The Wormwood Wind

Trills of April, singing cornices,
A whisper of leaves, the chirping of birds, kids!

26.09.2014

Raushan Burkitbayeva-Nukenova

To K. Balmont

The day, saying goodbye to me, has vanished in sorrow,
Passing motives have vanished in sorrow.
The evening, like a fellow, being sad,
Being sad - was first to picked up the motif.

Through the thinning darkness of the tired garden
Fruits of the tired garden were getting transparent.
And, it would seem the night was glad of this restful period
Was glad for this period of rest - to sum up its works.

The morning will come again with its frank smile,
Its frank smile will touch the day-chevalier.
It will pick up this fragile and shaky motif,
A fragile and shaky tea leaf from espaliers.

The infusion will thicken, acquiring bitterness.
Acquiring the bitterness of passed times.
Alone in the night, echoing to the deceased,
The rustling of old names echos to the deceased.

Day, saying goodbye to me, will vanish in sorrow,
This passing motif will vanish in sorrow.
And the end has turned out to be at the beginning,
It turned out to be at the beginning
without having asked us

14.09.2014

The Wormwood Wind

To Maurice Simashko

You've quenched our thirst and hunger,
Steered caravans of people.
And dissolved the cold of indifference
In a hot web of destinies, ideas.
Your word is the light chasing away darkness,
A song murmuring along the ditch,
The mystery of the East disclosed again,
Like an old man's prayer at the Walls.
With eternal longing for the Promised Land
You talked like Baybars for the call of the heart, the soul.
You are our welcomed friend - a guest to every home,
An admirer hurries to your books.
In time of troubles - peace and hope.
Like a revelation of the father-sage.
Your paroemia - as modern as ever.
Captivate us without end.
In each paragraph there is an ellipsis ...
There are so many versions and untold words.
Your sharpened Kalam is seeking the truth.
Maurice Simashko is a poet (the Prophet), Theologian! ..

13.10.2007

Astana for meeting of PEN club

Raushan Burkitbayeva-Nukenova

***

To A. Ermek

The canvas of a dazed river is speckling -
There is an extravaganza of pompous buildings
and fashion.
Our capital is being erected in the wilderness,
 like a movie.
Houses are blinding with mother of pearl.
While, this swarm of builders bothers the banks.
We hurry for jogging: we chase the morning.
Yet, the river hides its dream, like a snail.
And skiers are rumpling its numb back.
And a fountain gushes out in the summer.
Large-scale shooting will absorb picture stories -
reflecting the sunrise.
Bridges are sparkling and (with a rainbow of light),
spark lovers' hearts.
Rocking on waves under the sail of summer.
There will be no end to songs over the river!

Astana, 04.03.2009

The Wormwood Wind

***

A lantern with a black eye is hanging over
My blind window.
Tormented by fear, caustic gas -
Our city is enfolded by a dark dream.
Like mice in a dead faint,
Clouds are flying in a flock,
The uninhabited roofs are lightly touched
with rain - so far.
Fewer birds are in my yard,
Melancholy has increased twice.
Strong bolts are on the fence,
Where are birds killed, in war?
And the lantern with a black eye
Is hanging, with a tricky question.
The city gives roses in vases,
While looking down like a bat.
A century is twisted in double helix -
There is a sea of temptations awaiting you.
But the light is brighter behind an early distance,
It is the sunset of a rapid day ...

***

Wind - a wanderer, a pilgrim,
You are, like me, harassed by melancholy.
And you are flying, drawn by a dream,
To far unfamiliar lands,
Where you will find a love shelter.
Where you are, like a feast, long awaited.

Wind - a wanderer, a pilgrim,
You are my companion : blood brother.
We are rushing out in spite of fate
Along a path full of turns and twists.
I appreciate your participation,
We will find peace and happiness.

Wind - a wanderer, a pilgrim,
You are guarded by hope.
Escaping from pursuit,
We are carried away by frisky horses
Through hopes, gossip,
Through hardships and quirks.

In that mysterious country,
In the spring of pearl,
A delicate cherry colour is waiting,
That looks reproachfully after us,
Where gay thrushes
Tear ruthless flowers.

The Wormwood Wind

Wind - a wanderer, a pilgrim,
I am a servant, you are a master.
And a love like a mistress,
So naive and fresh
Fascinating endlessly
Because of passionate hearts!

Raushan Burkitbayeva-Nukenova

***

This life seems to me like a voice,
Through half asleep curtains of winter.
"What's it probing at in my heart, fighting?"
All this fear of otherworldly darkness.
At the end, what will be left - a handful of ash,
The attendance record and a grade book with erased F grades.
And our great-grandchildren will not care for us.
While my locomotive-twin will come to naught.
Only tired stars fall off hooks,
And fall down into the darkness after me.
Eternity will smile spitefully after it.
I will hug it, my friend!
Oh, imperishable light, like the voice of a captivating silence,
And rosy dawn's silky hair drawn by a snowdrifts of dreams!
This life seems to me like a voice...

Season of love

Oh, how the sweet cherry tree showed off,
Teasing passersby with a crimson colour.
Filled with winy juice
It had fun this summer.
An emerald fan of leaves
It did nothing to cool the fires of passion.
And greedy lips begged
It about absolute power.
And branches denuded noisely
And shades scattered in the garden...
And like a symphony of oblivion,
Lilac leaves trembled.

Rain

It flies from unimaginable heights,
From a far distance.
And its life, all the time, is flying,
Like the circle of grief.
It will be broken easily,
Without regret.
And will become a drop in a pond
Or a wet shadow.
Or the moist soil -
For a fragile sprout
Rising up proudly from the dust
With a dear smile.

Our sea

The beach is licking persistently at our heels.
Its waves heal our wounds.
The day will dash off, like a dream,
without looking back.
At night, you'll be alone again.
Flocks are echoing as a leaving line.
Footprints disappear in the sand.
The ringing bracelet on a thin hand
Demands a memory of happy hours.
Fascinated by a wonderful melody,
Yet, the evening surf calms down.
And it is so difficult to forget that sea,
Take it with you like collected shells.

Raushan Burkitbayeva-Nukenova

Epicrisis

Hello Spring, young nurse!
Come in boldly! Wide open doors, windows.
A handful of freckles, pigtails under the cap,
Splash your laughter in a sentimental wine!
Let plain appearance, neighborhood diaper rash
Be covered quickly by the day flower bliss.
Come in like a holiday, with long-awaited charm!
Everyone is so tired of the stagnant snow.
Dance, my sun, ring with the streams.
The wind caresses with a tulip infusion.
And we must blame ourselves for long depressions.
Everyone deserves love and sympathy.
Desires are like drippings, let them be funny
and sinful.
A passerbys face is confused by a smile,
So tired - waiting for a miracle.
But, our hearts are wounded by loss and pain.
A diagnosis is made – we should treat it with love!

Metamorphoses

Whether due to jealousy,
Whether due to joy -
Silver drops,
Dragees of chords
Are scattered by rain
One day is bitterness, the other sweetness
In frenzied dances of
Love, in virage.
The warm speeches of
A gentle wind
A garden wrapped in dreams
Like a sweet drink.
And having prepared for
A joyful meeting,
Trees are dressed
In bridal array.
Rain is tired;
And I am stunned.
For a week, forgetting myself,
Having searched for a miracle.
Having thrown off the captivity
Of shapeless pants-
Female legs covered with Lycra
Beckoning our glances,
Like blossomed apricots.
Girls are flying in
An enthusiastic flock!

Raushan Burkitbayeva-Nukenova

***

This short summer is fading away,
The garden is chilled by wind.
An admiring glance remembers
So many colours, so much light.
It is cold in the forgotten house,
Birds have already gone south.
Into an abysmal, open sky-
There is fright within a mature autumn.
In long silences the word is
Fermenting like the dawn after night.
There is neither minor, nor major,
Yet, nothing is impossible either.
With each loss, it is more precious
A thing that cannot be caught up.
We were younger and hasher back then,
And did not know how to forgive.
And the floorboard creaked,
Like starling-houses in delirium.
Listen, tits has started singing
In our May flowering garden!

Conservatory

An invisible bird is cawking in the night.
And a white garden is lulling the moon.
You're enjoying a balmy sleep.
The night is melting on your eyelashes.
Lilac is floating to an open window.
Couples are tirelessly dancing by the clock,
Where the pendulum is performing its long duty.
A tired star will dive into an old well,
Oversleeping its harmonious lessons.
Ear training, ballet, diet, dancing.
But how may we calm an anxious heart beat?
Foreign guests have fallen into the habit of visiting you.
And your timetable for the year – like a sentence
Of life imprisonment. I'm afraid of looking at it.
I'll run away with spring rain to the mountains, anyway,
I'll fall in love with you without permission!

05.05.2009

Raushan Burkitbayeva-Nukenova

"Umai" Gallery

A ghostly fire of fallen leaves ...
I'm cold, it won't warm me up.
A footworn carpet clings to my feet
I'm wandering alone in a hushed gallery.
Dust is falling across ancient arts.
And my sadnes is like a veil of rain.
This does not inspire the old stories
Or the glances of a radiant leader.

***

By a strong coffee cup of love,
By a fancy crispy croissant in the morning,
Paris - waiter, do not ruin my dream!
Curtain the window with a flowering chestnut.
Kiss a glass of champagne slightly,
Stay in the shower like a singing Montmartre.
Like the River Seine run through my years -
In the paintings of Monet, pop art sketches.
Melancholy – like a scraper on the parquet of Caillebotte
Fly to the Moulin Rouge, to the Latin neighborhood,
When you're lonely, when you're exhausted.
 (Henry) de Toulouse-Lautrec whiled away his days there.
As garlands of hurrying night taxis.
Drive through a poison of sophisticated gourmet tastes.
Cooks are doing magic for them, "Sorry!" - "Mercy!".
Cafes chantants splashe with a river of love!

The Eiffel Tower

Beyond the smoky veil of rain
The Eiffel Tower is hiding like a lady.
"Cherchez la femme!" – buzzing like a bumble bee.
They go crazily for the scaffold of Love!
And at night it lights up
Twined with chains of fire.
It is visible from the windows of each hotel,
Piercing the sky-heart, like a needle,
Flying proudly in the sky, "Voila!"
Sent down like a delicate steel lace
People (like lice) teem about it.
Legions of rains, winds, centuries.
Meet the delight of love - "SOS" signals.
With an elusive scarf of perfume
It is crowned by this immortality elixir.
Mufflers of chestnuts and a liqueur of sins -
All in pairs – in intimate "Mon Plaisir". ***

Raushan Burkitbayeva-Nukenova

Parisian

The flicker of rain is like a string of pearls -
Through the Arc de Triomphe- in a balletic manner!
And Parisians are dressed in a perfume tail,
Along the Champs-Elysees - to a first date!
A murmur of delighted plane trees,
And glances, the admiration of passersby.
Frame her sadness to look like
A mist - from steaming chestnuts,
A lace of violets.
She will look so innocent, mandarin-like
Through the veil of her painted lashes.
Like a thin frost web laid on the heart.
She will be in my dreams for a long time.
Will be fluffing like a poplar distress.
Well, tell me how not to fall in love with her!

Umbrellas of Cherbourg

Catherine Deneuve, Michel Legrand
And the music of rains-
Will heal the wounds of the heart,
Chill, tears, ideas.
Beyond the outstretched horizon,
Opening an umbrella like wings.
Flying from wet, slippery roofs,
You are flying, singing, hovering.
And sunsets are slowly smoldering
With a mystic fire.
Hugged with the anesthesia caress of sleep
That house – a ship is sailing.
Let's skip across to Paris!

Impressionism - Claude Monet

Like in mystery
>   Drawdows enter in.
Passing times
>   Change faces, masks.
In the depths of the water
>   We are immersed by colors,
And the world
>   Sparkles by shades!
Water Lilies are
>   On the pond surface ...
Oh, how much work ! -
>   Did it take.
You in open air
>   Dug a trench,
To grasp the shadow of light
>   By a neck turn.
And the pearl of the sun
>   Is lost in the folds of a dress!
Wind gusts are -
>   In trembling arms.
Breathy flowers are
>   In a greenhouse fog.
Poppies are blushing,
>   Sluffing amongst herbs.
FThe fickering signs of -
>   Forbidden words!

The Wormwood Wind

Your umbrella is
> Floating in the wine of centuries.
Palettes of feelings are -
> A bright inflorescence!

Impressionism from impression (French)
23-24.12.2014

Raushan Burkitbayeva-Nukenova

Paris Street

I suspect Paris of foul play,
When I stray in the narrow streets -
In a huddle ... as in a net – trapped
It entices whispering compliments in your ear.
Tobacco smoke having thrown a cobweb
Of smiles like a clown – leads the mime to me.
And sophisticated perfumer Chanel
Decorates Mademoiselle with rain-tears.   .
But, a provincial night is clinging to the roof,
It does not want to leave: "I want to sojourn in Paris!"
Oh, I understand it like my girl friend
I sympathy, listen to all the arguments.
Ecxelling so, and making eyes,
Calls for gratitude, for kindness.
Ah, sycamore has drooped, having whispered by its foliage.
It has stretched out branches over the pavement.
Waiting on a boulevard - looking into the windows of
Cafes and restaurants. We will get wet,
Slide on the faces of weary streets,
Breathing the smell of fresh buns!

Shocking by Elsa Schiaparelli

Wrapped up in a black coat,
Clapping on a hat like a cloud.
You – like a soaked rose - in the car
Are hurring through the night,
where awaits - Dali! Cocteau!
Fireworks of the fantasy, the outrageous!
The grotesque! - Prizes! – To Windsor Castle
A dress is a still life, collage salad.
... Your hat is crawling…under a shoe.
A lobster in delirium has wandered to the hem.
I will find flared trousers in your wardrobe.
I will erase my sketch with an rubber.
Fuchsia has decorated a lipstick!
Torso - a bottle of perfume, an ultimate dream!
Not a sofa - but a kiss for a butt.
You are a nightmare for prudish Europe!
"Podium is not a place for clownery!"
Your triumph is predicted by fate.
Your outfits are snapped up.
Everyone is shocked!
You are tearing up reality in canvases!

May-bugs

Over a May garden's white foam -
There are flights of buzzing bugs.
Purple smoke is over the fence
And the meadows' have a tender greenery.
And willows' swirling in play,
Hide and seek with cheer.
Nectar is collected by beetles,
Fatigue is a piece of cake for them!
And is it love's fault,
That you have forgotten it?
A day with an Asian's cunning,
Sailed contented with its tribute.
Over a May garden's white foam -

There are bronze beetles.
Don't poison them
With the venom of unnecessary anguish.

***

The night has brought a long-awaited coolness,
The wind dozed among branches.
The moonlight has penetrated through a fence,
Merged with the fragrance of orchids.

***

Oh, how am I so far from you?
Where is my coveted flower?
Who drinks its gentle nectar?
Is it full of former charms?

Raushan Burkitbayeva-Nukenova

Snowafall

Like a cold of temptation -
The snow is falling, and falling.
It is light at first,
And does blind!
Yet, I'm afraid of getting stuck in it,
But it still descends.
Persistent and lingering.
It seemed it was celebrating
A light victory.
For our bored city
Having surrendered to this siege.
The snow will go down by dinner-time
And the wind too
Will chase it away -
But such thoughts were vain,
Dangerous inventions.
It seemed to me
It did not pretend.
Like a dream, an obsession
That was a convergence
Of something different
Something great -
A second birth?
Poems torn down
By a snow storm
Have broken the peace.
Snowflakes will seduce

The Wormwood Wind

Will swoop, out of the blue
Will stick all over us like flies.
Ah, that desired captivity!
Ice-slick and rumors…
Ah, how to avoid breaking
Ah, how to avoid falling in love!
The snow is getting thicker and thicker.
It will start turning, swirling into a snowstorm
Turning us in the dance.
Of a whitened darkness, night.
Tailing fear
Calling in the blackness
Frost sticks like a glue tape
A line of towsy
Pine-trees are left silent
Slightly powdered,
Thrown away by the snowstorm.
Like an unbidden guest,
Inverting the world
Inspired love in us
Having filled itself
With a thick curtain
Of snow renewing life!
It is falling, and falling…

08.12.2014

Raushan Burkitbayeva-Nukenova

***

A tram ski-track
Is ringing with its drippings!
Where in the music of parting?
This neighbourhood has fallen asleep.
Yet, the winter will pass away
In a hasty fuss,
After all, the starling has already chirruped!
And sand grains keep
 The opinions of wisdom.
Children's laughter
 Is speeding like an arrow.
While a lilac fragrance
 Is wafting through the garden,
And there is no end -
To the tram way!

2012

Praying

When the star of love shines in the blueness,
And an enthusiastic cricket signs in the grass.
Dreams of a busy day calm down.
 Call me! Call me!

Like gentle rays mid weird darkness,
Spring flowers hurry after the warmth.
Together with a growing moon
Along the rainbow pathway
I will fly to you! I will fly to you!

Look at the window - there is a circling star dance
As every day meets each blushing sunrise.
Do not lose hope, even if this life is a struggle.
Let destiny keep him! Let destiny keep him!

But remember, how short is an instant of the glorious day.
Carrousel flies ringing round with delight -
Earlier eagerness will burn out, but not my love .
What goes around, comes around!
What goes around, comes around!

Raushan Burkitbayeva-Nukenova

***

Poems will come!
Like May thunderstorms come
The Universe is singing
 In the handfull of sand!
A wife-poet, like a thorn
In her husband's flesh.
 She floats like a mist
Among stars.
In one instant
There is eternities vexation.
An ocean raging in dew tears!
Is it a punishment
Or luck to someone?
Life is a short dream,
Illusion, deceit.
Compress the answer to
The comma in a notebook.
By one stroke - the palette of all centuries.
Does not disturb the poet,
For Heaven's sake!
He escaped from himself
By his poems.
In the snows of the night,
In the Tibetan backwoods.
In the taiga and tundra-
He is hurrying to his friends.
Polishing his style indefatigably

The Wormwood Wind

Like a blessed truth.
While a flame is burning –
In the fire of his soul!

12.12.2014

Burkitbayeva - Nukenova Raushan

Raushan Burkitbayeva-Nukenova's was born in July 20, 1956 in Taraz city, in the Zhambyl Region, to a family of teachers.

In 1980, she graduated with honors from the Karaganda State Medical University, Sanitary and Hygienic department. Upon completion of her degree, she worked as a medical officer, bacteriologist and epidemiologist in the system of Sanitary and Epidemiological Stations of Almaty city and the Almaty region.

In parallel to her primary occupation, she was engaged in creative activities. Raushan is the author of more than 10 books published in Kazakhstan, Russia, and France. Nukenova's titles include, "I envy the Sun" (1996), "The arabesques of love" (1996), "Love - a nomad" (1998), "Night mirrors" (Almaty, 2001), "The mystery of night" (Moscow, 2002), "The berth of dreams" (Moscow, 2006), "The embankment of hopes" (Moscow, 2006) - "Le qual de tous les espoirs" (Paris, 2014), "The rock drawings - Peintures rupestres" (Paris, 2015), etc., as well as prose.

Since 1973, she has also published in the regional newspaper "Znamya Truda" in Dzhambul city. Additionally, she has contributed to the district newspaper of Kaskelen town and a student newspaper "For health care personnel", "Business and Finances", "Evening Astana", "Time", "NP", as well as in journals "Business woman", "East-West woman", Almanac "Literary Alma-ata", "Amanat", "Oner", "Yunost'" (Mscow, 2002-2009) Innterestingly, more than 30 songs were developed, in poetry collections "Pearl poetry of Kazakhstan", "Your name..." (Finland), "The fiery Stalingrad" (2013), "Life pages of L. Iu. Girsh" (2014), etc. She played in "The alley of poets" films, and the serialized television programme "Culture" on the Khabar, Caspionet and Rakhat TV channels.

Five of Raushan's writings have been included in a textbook anthology on Self-discovery for 8th grade students. Equally, she is the author of anthems for Financial Police and

Customs. Innterestingly, more than 30 songs were developed based on Raushan's poems by E. Shakeev, E. Khasangaliev, B. Oralbekov composers, etc.

In 2008, the Moscow publishing house "Ripol Classic" published her book "The face of the escaping moon" within the serias of entitled "Altar of poetry".

Raushan Burkitbayeva-Nukenova is a laureate of the international poetry competition named after Abai.

She is an Honored Arts Worker of Kazakhstan (2011), member of the Writers' Union of Kazakhstan (2008), member of the International Pen-club (2007), member of Poetas del Mundo (Paris, 2014). Raushan lives and works in Almaty.

HERTFORDSHIRE PRESS

Title List

Igor Savitsky:
Artist, Collector, Museum Founder
by Marinika Babanazarova (2011)

Since the early 2000s, Igor Savitsky's life and accomplishments have earned increasing international recognition. He and the museum he founded in Nukus, the capital of Karakalpakstan in the far northwest of Uzbekistan. Marinika Babanazarova's memoir is based on her 1990 graduate dissertation at the Tashkent Theatre and Art Institute. It draws upon correspondence, official records, and other documents about the Savitsky family that have become available during the last few years, as well as the recollections of a wide range of people who knew Igor Savitsky personally.

Игорь Савитский: художник, собиратель, основатель музея

С начала 2000-х годов, жизнь и достижения Игоря Савицкого получили широкое признание во всем мире. Он и его музей, основанный в Нукусе, столице Каракалпакстана, стали предметом многочисленных статей в мировых газетах и журналах, таких как TheGuardian и NewYorkTimes, телевизионных программ в Австралии, Германии и Японии. Книга издана на русском, английском и французском языках.

Igor Savitski: Peintre, collectionneur, fondateur du Musée (French), (2012)

Le mémoire de Mme Babanazarova, basé sur sa thèse de 1990 à l'Institut de Théâtre et D'art de Tachkent, s'appuie sur la correspondance, les dossiers officiels et d'autres documents d'Igor Savitsky et de sa famille, qui sont devenus disponibles dernièrement, ainsi que sur les souvenirs de nombreuses personnes ayant connu Savistky personellement, ainsi que sur sa propre expérience de travail a ses cotés, en tant que successeur designé. son nom a titre posthume.

LANGUAGE: **ENG, RUS, FR**   ISBN: **978-0955754999**   RRP: **£10.00**
AVAILABLE ON **KINDLE**

Savitsky Collection Selected Masterpieces.
Poster set of 8 posters (2014)

Limited edition of prints from the world-renowned Museum of Igor
Savitsky in Nukus, Uzbekistan. The set includs nine of the most famous
works from the Savitsky collection wrapped in a colourful envelope.
Selected Masterpieces of the Savitsky Collection.

[Cover] BullVasily Lysenko 1. Oriental Café Aleksei Isupov
2. Rendezvous Sergei Luppov 3. By the Sea. Marie-LouiseKliment
Red'ko 4. Apocalypse Aleksei Rybnikov 5. Rain Irina Shtange 6. Purple
Autumn Ural Tansykbayaev 7. To the Train Viktor Ufimtsev 8. Brigade
to the fields Alexander Volkov This museum, also known as the Nukus
Museum or the Savitsky

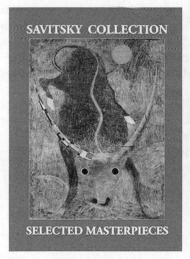
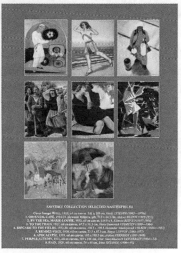

ISBN: **9780992787387**
RRP: **£25.00**

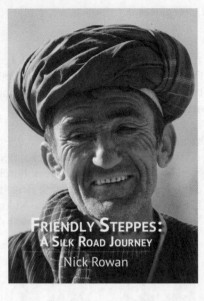

Friendly Steppes.
A Silk Road Journey
by Nick Rowan

This is the chronicle of an extraordinary adventure that led Nick Rowan to some of the world's most incredible and hidden places. Intertwined with the magic of 2,000 years of Silk Road history, he recounts his experiences coupled with a remarkable realisation of just what an impact this trade route has had on our society as we know it today. Containing colourful stories, beautiful photography and vivid characters, and wrapped in the local myths and legends told by the people Nick met and who live along the route, this is both a travelogue and an education of a part of the world that has remained hidden for hundreds of years.

HARD BACK ISBN: **978-0-9927873-4-9**
PAPERBACK ISBN: **978-0-9557549-4-4**
RRP: **£14.95**
AVAILABLE ON **KINDLE**

Birds of Uzbeksitan
by Nedosekov (2012)

FIRST
AND ONLY PHOTOALBUM
OF UZBEKISTAN BIRDS!

This book, which provides an introduction to the birdlife of Uzbekistan, is a welcome addition to the tools available to those working to conserve the natural heritage of the country. In addition to being the first photographic guide to the birds of Uzbekistan, the book is unique in only using photographs taken within the country. The compilers arc to be congratulated on preparing an attractive and accessible work which hopefully will encourage more people to discover the rich birdlife of the country and want to protect it for future generations

HARD BACK
ISBN: **978-0-955754913**
RRP: **£25.00**

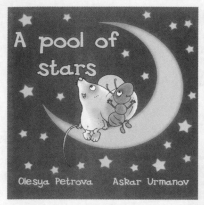

Pool of Stars
by Olesya Petrova,
Askar Urmanov,
English Edition (2007)

It is the first publication of a young writer Olesya Petrova, a talented and creative person. Fairy-tale characters dwell on this book's pages. Lovely illustrations make this book even more interesting to kids, thanks to a remarkable artist Askar Urmanov. We hope that our young readers will be very happy with such a gift. It's a book that everyone will appreciate. For the young, innocent ones - it's a good source of lessons they'll need in life. For the not-so-young but young at heart, it's a great book to remind us that life is so much more than work.

ISBN: **978-0955754906** **ENGLISH** AVAILABLE ON **KINDLE**

«Звёздная лужица»

Первая книга для детей, изданная британским издательством Hertfordshire Press. Это также первая публикация молодой талантливой писательницы Олеси Петровой. Сказочные персонажи живут на страницах этой книги. Прекрасные иллюстрации делают книгу еще более интересной и красочной для детей, благодаря замечательному художнику Аскару Урманову. Вместе Аскар и Олеся составляют удивительный творческий тандем, который привнес жизнь в эту маленькую книгу

ISBN: **978-0955754906** **RUSSIAN**
RRP: **£4.95**

Buyuk Temurhon (Tamerlane)
by C. Marlowe,
Uzbek Edition (2010)

Hertfordshire based publisher Silk Road Media, run by Marat Akhmedjanov, and the BBC Uzbek Service have published one of Christopher Marlowe's famous plays, Tamburlaine the Great, translated into the Uzbek language. It is the first of Christopher Marlowe's plays to be translated into Uzbek, which is Tamburlaine's native language. Translated by Hamid Ismailov, the current BBC World Service Writer-in-Residence, this new publication seeks to introduce English classics to Uzbek readers worldwide.

PAPERBACK
ISBN: **9780955754982**
RRP: **£10.00**
AVAILABLE ON **KINDLE**

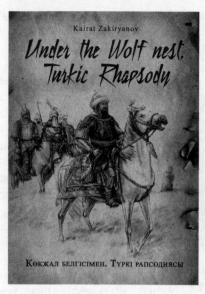

Kairat Zakiryanov

Under the Wolf nest.
Turkic Rhapsody

Көкжал белгісімен. Түркі рапсодиясы

Under Wolf's Nest
by KairatZakiryanov
English –Kazakh edition

Were the origins of Islam, Christianity and the legend of King Arthur all influenced by steppe nomads from Kazakhstan? Ranging through thousands of years of history, and drawing on sources from Herodotus through to contemporary Kazakh and Russian research, the crucial role in the creation of modern civilisation played by the Turkic people is revealed in this detailed yet highly accessible work. Professor Kairat Zakiryanov, President of the Kazakh Academy of Sport and Tourism, explains how generations of steppe nomads, including Genghis Khan, have helped shape the language, culture and populations of Asia, Europe, the Middle East and America through migrations taking place over millennia.

HARD BACK
ISBN: **9780957480728**
RRP: **£17.50**
AVAILABLE ON **KINDLE**

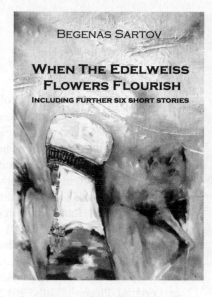

When Edelweiss flowers flourish
by Begenas Saratov
English edition (2012)

A spectacular insight into life in the Soviet Union in the late 1960's made all the more intriguing by its setting within the Sovet Republic of Kyrgyzstan. The story explores Soviet life, traditional Kyrgyz life and life on planet Earth through a Science Fiction story based around an alien nations plundering of the planet for life giving herbs. The author reveals far sighted thoughts and concerns for conservation, management of natural resources and dialogue to achieve peace yet at the same time shows extraordinary foresight with ideas for future technologies and the progress of science. The whole style of the writing gives a fascinating insight into the many facets of life in a highly civilised yet rarely known part of the world.

ISBN: **978-0955754951** **PAPERBACK** AVAILABLE ON **KINDLE**

Mamyry gyldogon maalda

Это фантастический рассказ, повествующий о советской жизни, жизни кыргызского народа и о жизни на планете в целом. Автор рассказывает об инопланетных народах, которые пришли на нашу планету, чтобы разграбить ее. Автор раскрывает дальновидность мысли о сохранение и рациональном использовании природных ресурсов, а также диалога для достижения мира и в то же время показывает необычайную дальновидность с идеями для будущих технологий и прогресса науки. Книга также издана на **кыргызском языке**.

ISBN: **9780955754951**
RRP: **£12.95**

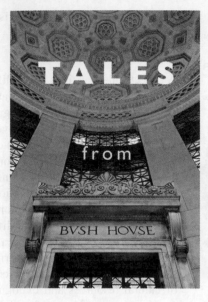

Tales from Bush House
(BBC Wolrd Service)
by Hamid Ismailov
(2012)

Tales From Bush House is a collection of short narratives about working lives, mostly real and comic, sometimes poignant or apocryphal, gifted to the editors by former and current BBC World Service employees. They are tales from inside Bush House - the home of the World Service since 1941 - escaping through its marble-clad walls at a time when its staff begin their departure to new premises in Portland Place. In July 2012, the grand doors of this imposing building will close on a vibrant chapter in the history of Britain's most cosmopolitan organisation. So this is a timely book.

PAPERBACK
ISBN: **9780955754975**
RRP: **£12.95**
AVAILABLE ON **KINDLE**

Chants of Dark Fire
(Песни темного огня)
by Zhulduz Baizakova
Russian edition (2012)

This contemporary work of poetry contains the deep and inspirational rhythms of the ancient Steppe. It combines the nomad, modern, postmodern influences in Kazakhstani culture in the early 21st century, and reveals the hidden depths of contrasts, darkness, and longing for light that breathes both ice and fire to inspire a rich form of poetry worthy of reading and contemplating. It is also distinguished by the uniqueness of its style and substance. Simply sublime, it has to be read and felt for real.

ISBN: **978-0957480711**
RRP: **£10.00**

Kamila
by R. Karimov
Kyrgyz – Uzbek Edition (2013)

«Камила» - это история о сироте,
растущей на юге Кыргызстана.
Наряду с личной трагедией
Камилы и ее родителей, Рахим
Каримов описывает очень
реалистично и подробно
местный образ жизни. Роман
выиграл конкурс "Искусство
книги-2005" в Бишкеке
и был признан национальным
бестселлером Книжной палаты
Кыргызской Республики.

PAPERBACK
ISBN: **978-0957480773**
RRP: **£10.00**

Gods of the Middle World
by Galina Dolgaya (2013)

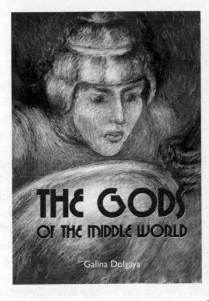

The Gods of the Middle World tells the story of Sima, a student of archaeology for whom the old lore and ways of the Central Asian steppe peoples are as vivid as the present. When she joints a group of archaeologists in southern Kazakhstan, asking all the time whether it is really possible to 'commune with the spirits', she soon discovers the answer first hand, setting in motion events in the spirit world that have been frozen for centuries. Meanwhile three millennia earlier, on the same spot, a young woman and her companion struggle to survive and amend wrongs that have caused the neighbouring tribe to take revenge. The two narratives mirror one another, and Sima's destiny is to resolve the ancient wrongs in her own lifetime and so restore the proper balance of the forces of good and evil

PAPERBACK
ISBN: **978-0957480797**
RRP: **£14.95**
AVAILABLE ON **KINDLE**

13 steps of Erika Klaus
by Kazat Akmatov (2013)

The story involves the harrowing experiences of a young and very naïve Norwegian woman who has come to Kyrgyzstan to teach English to schoolchildren in a remote mountain outpost. Governed by the megalomaniac Colonel Bronza, the community barely survives under a cruel and unjust neo-fascist regime. Immersed in the local culture, Erika is initially both enchanted and apprehensive but soon becomes disillusioned as day after day, she is forbidden to teach. Alongside Erika's story, are the personal tragedies experienced by former soldier Sovietbek , Stalbek, the local policeman, the Principal of the school and a young man who has married a Kyrgyz refugee from Afghanistan . Each tries in vain, to challenge and change the corrupt political situation in which they are forced to live.

PAPERBACK
ISBN: **978-0957480766**
RRP: **£12.95**
AVAILABLE ON **KINDLE**

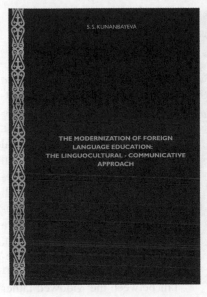

The Modernization of Foreign Language Education: The Linguocultural - Communicative Approach
by SalimaKunanbayeva (2013)

Professor S. S. Kunanbayeva - Rector of Ablai Khan Kazakh University of International Relations and World Languages This textbook is the first of its kind in Kazakhstan to be devoted to the theory and practice of foreign language education. It has been written primarily for future teachers of foreign languages and in a wider sense for all those who to be interested in the question (in the problems?) of the study and use of foreign languages. This book outlines an integrated theory of modern foreign language learning (FLL) which has been drawn up and approved under the auspices of the school of science and methodology of Kazakhstan's Ablai Khan University of International Relations and World Languages.

PAPERBACK
ISBN: **978-0957480780**
RRP: **£19.95**
AVAILABLE ON **KINDLE**

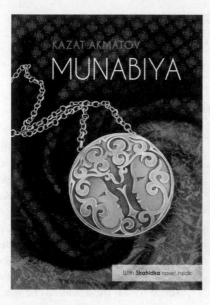

Shahidka/ Munabia
by KazatAkmatov (2013)

Munabiya and Shahidka by Kazat Akmatov National Writer of Kyrgyzstan Recently translated into English Akmatov's two love stories are set in rural Kyrgyzstan, where the natural environment, local culture, traditions and political climate all play an integral part in the dramas which unfold. Munabiya is a tale of a family's frustration, fury, sadness and eventual acceptance of a long term love affair between the widowed father and his mistress. In contrast, Shahidka is a multi-stranded story which focuses on the ties which bind a series of individuals to the tragic and ill-fated union between a local Russian girl and her Chechen lover, within a multi-cultural community where violence, corruption and propaganda are part of everyday life.

PAPERBACK
ISBN: **978-0957480759**
RRP: **£12.95**
AVAILABLE ON **KINDLE**

Бонус! Новеллы "Вой" и "Мунабия" на русском языке

Howl *novel*
by Kazat Akmatov (2014)
English –Russian

The "Howl" by Kazat Akmatov is a beautifully crafted novel centred on life in rural Kyrgyzstan. Characteristic of the country's national writer, the simple plot is imbued with descriptions of the spectacular landscape, wildlife and local customs. The theme however, is universal and the contradictory emotions experienced by Kalen the shepherd must surely ring true to young men, and their parents, the world over. Here is a haunting and sensitively written story of a bitter -sweet rite of passage from boyhood to manhood.

PAPERBACK
ISBN: **978-0993044410**
RRP: **£12.50**
AVAILABLE ON **KINDLE**

KAIRAT ZAKIRYANOV

THE TURKIC SAGA OF GENGHIS KHAN AND THE KZ FACTOR

**The Turkic Saga
of Genghis Khan
and the KZ Factor**
by Dr.Kairat Zakiryanov (2014)

An in-depth study of Genghis Khan from a Kazakh perspective, The Turkic Saga of Genghis Khan presupposes that the great Mongol leader and his tribal setting had more in common with the ancestors of the Kazakhs than with the people who today identify as Mongols. This idea is growing in currency in both western and eastern scholarship and is challenging both old Western assumptions and the long-obsolete Soviet perspective. This is an academic work that draws on many Central Asian and Russian sources and often has a Eurasianist bias - while also paying attention to new accounts by Western authors such as Jack Weatherford and John Man. It bears the mark of an independent, unorthodox and passionate scholar.

HARD BACK
ISBN: **978-0992787370**
RRP: **£17.50**
AVAILABLE ON **KINDLE**

Alphabet Game
by Paul Wilson (2014)

Travelling around the world may appear as easy as ABC, but looks can be deceptive: there is no 'X' for a start. Not since Xidakistan was struck from the map. Yet post 9/11, with the War on Terror going global, could 'The Valley' be about to regain its place on the political stage? Xidakistan's fate is inextricably linked with that of Graham Ruff, founder of Ruff Guides. Setting sail where Around the World in Eighty Days and Lost Horizon weighed anchor, our not-quite-a-hero suffers all in pursuit of his golden triangle: The Game, The Guidebook, The Girl. With the future of printed Guidebooks increasingly in question, As Evelyn Waugh's Scoop did for Foreign Correspondents the world over, so this novel lifts the lid on Travel Writers for good.

PAPERBACK
ISBN: **978-0-992787325**
RRP: **£14.95**
AVAILABLE ON **KINDLE**

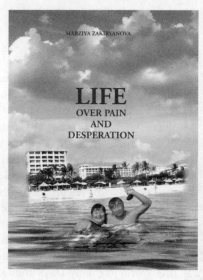

Life over pain and desperation
by Marziya Zakiryanova (2014)

This book was written by someone on the fringe of death. Her life had been split in two: before and after the first day of August 1991 when she, a mother of two small children and full of hopes and plans for the future, became disabled in a single twist of fate. Narrating her tale of self-conquest, the author speaks about how she managed to hold her family together, win the respect and recognition of people around her and above all, protect the fragile concept of 'love' from fortune's cruel turns. By the time the book was submitted to print, Marziya Zakiryanova had passed away. She died after making the last correction to her script. We bid farewell to this remarkable and powerfully creative woman.

HARD BACK
ISBN: **978-0-99278733-2**
RRP: **£14.95**
AVAILABLE ON **KINDLE**

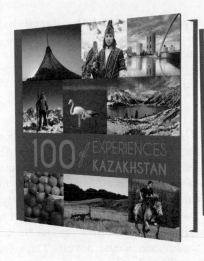

100 experiences
of Kazakhstan
by Vitaly Shuptar, Nick Rowan
and Dagmar Schreiber (2014)

The original land of the nomads, landlocked Kazakhstan
and its expansive steppes present an intriguing border between Europe and Asia. Dis-
pel the notion of oil barons
and Borat and be prepared
for a warm welcome into a land
full of contrasts. A visit to this
newly independent country
will transport you to a bygone era to discover a country full of legends and wonders. Whether searching for the descendants of Genghis
Khan - who left his mark on this land seven hundred years ago -
or looking to discover the futuristic architecture of its capital Astana, visitors cannot fail but be impressed by what they experience.
For those seeking adventure, the formidable Altai and Tien Shan
mountains provide challenges for novices and experts alike

ISBN: **978-0-992787356**
RRP: **£19.95**

Dance of Devils , Jinlar Bazmi
by AbdulhamidIsmoil
and Hamid Ismailov
(Uzbek language),
E-book (2012)

'Dance of Devils' is a novel about the life of a great Uzbek writer Abdulla Qadyri (incidentally, 'Dance of Devils' is the name of one of his earliest short stories). In 1937, Qadyri was going to write a novel, which he said was to make his readers to stop reading his iconic novels "Days Bygone" and "Scorpion from the altar," so beautiful it would have been. The novel would've told about a certain maid, who became a wife of three Khans - a kind of Uzbek Helen of Troy. He told everyone: "I will sit down this winter and finish this novel - I have done my preparatory work, it remains only to write. Then people will stop reading my previous books". He began writing this novel, but on the December 31, 1937 he was arrested.

AVAILABLE ON **KINDLE**
ASIN: B009ZBPV2M

Vanished Khans and Empty Steppes by Robert Wight (2014)

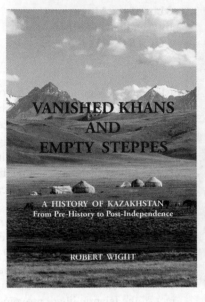

The book opens with an outline of the history of Almaty, from its nineteenth-century origins as a remote outpost of the Russian empire, up to its present status as the thriving second city of modern-day Kazakhstan. The story then goes back to the Neolithic and early Bronze Ages, and the sensational discovery of the famous Golden Man of the Scythian empire. The transition has been difficult and tumultuous for millions of people, but Vanished Khans and Empty Steppes illustrates how Kazakhstan has emerged as one of the world's most successful post-communist countries.

HARD BACK
ISBN: **978-0-9930444-0-3**
RRP: **£24.95**

PAPERBACK
ISBSN: **978-1-910886-05-2**
RRP: **£14.50**
AVAILABLE ON **KINDLE**

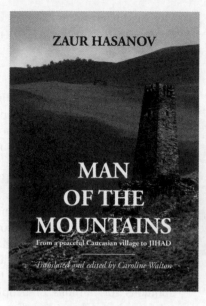

Man of the Mountains
by Abudlla Isa (2014)
(OCABF 2013 Winner)

Man of the Mountains" is a book about a young Muslim Chechen boy, Zaur who becomes a central figure representing the fight of local indigenous people against both the Russians invading the country and Islamic radicals trying to take a leverage of the situation, using it to push their narrow political agenda on the eve of collapse of the USSR. After 9/11 and the invasion of Iraq and Afghanistan by coalition forces, the subject of the Islamic jihadi movement has become an important subject for the Western readers. But few know about the resistance movement from the local intellectuals and moderates against radical Islamists taking strong hold in the area.

PAPERBACK
ISBN: **978-0-9930444-5-8**
RRP: **£14.95**
AVAILABLE ON **KINDLE**

Silk, Spice, Veils and Vodka
by Felicity Timcke (2014)

Felicity Timcke's missive publication, "Silk, Spices, Veils and Vodka" brings both a refreshing and new approach to life on the expat trail. South African by origin, Timcke has lived in some very exotic places, mostly along the more challenging countries of the Silk Road. Although the book's content, which is entirely composed of letters to the author's friends and family, is directed primarily at this group, it provides "20 years of musings" that will enthral and delight those who have either experienced a similar expatriate existence or who are nervously about to depart for one.

PAPERBACK
ISBN: **978-0992787318**
RRP: **£12.50**
AVAILABLE ON **KINDLE**

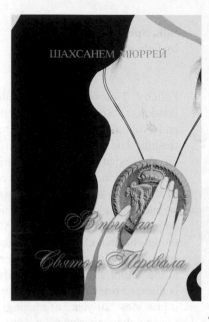

Finding the Holy Path
by Shahsanem Murray (2014)

"Murray's first book provides an enticing and novel link between her adopted home town of Edinburgh and her origins form Central Asia. Beginning with an investigation into a mysterious lamp that turns up in an antiques shop in Edinburgh, and is bought on impulse, we are quickly brought to the fertile Ferghana valley in Uzbekistan to witness the birth of Kara-Choro, and the start of an enthralling story that links past and present. Told through a vivid and passionate dialogue, this is a tale of parallel discovery and intrigue. The beautifully translated text, interspersed by regional poetry, cannot fail to impress any reader, especially those new to the region who will be affectionately drawn into its heart in this page-turning cultural thriller."

В поисках святого перевала – удивительный приключенческий роман, основанный на исторических источниках. Произведение Мюррей – это временной мостик между эпохами, который помогает нам переместиться в прошлое и уносит нас далеко в 16 век. Закрученный сюжет предоставляет нам уникальную возможность, познакомиться с историейи культурой Центральной Азии. «Первая книга Мюррей предлагает заманчивый роман, связывающий между её приемным городом Эдинбургом и Центральной Азией, откуда настоящее происхождение автора.

RUS ISBN: **978-0-9930444-8-9**
ENGL ISBN: **978-0992787394**
PAPERBACK
RRP: **£12.50**

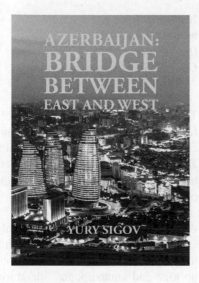

Azerbaijan:
Bridge between East and West
by Yury Sigov, 2015

Azerbaijan: Bridge between East and West, Yury Sigov narrates a comprehensive and compelling story about Azerbaijan. He balances the country's rich cultural heritage, wonderful people and vibrant environment with its modern political and economic strategies. Readers will get the chance to thoroughly explore Azerbaijan from many different perspectives and discover a plethora of innovations and idea, including the recipe for Azerbaijan's success as a nation and its strategies for the future. The book also explores the history of relationships between United Kingdom and Azerbaijan.

HARD BACK
ISBN: **978-0-9930444-9-6**
RRP: **£24.50**
AVAILABLE ON **KINDLE**

Kashmir Song
by Sharaf Rashidov
(translation by Alexey Ulko, OCABF 2014 Winner). 2015

This beautiful illustrated novella offers a sensitive reworking of an ancient and enchanting folk story which although rooted in Kashmir is, by nature of its theme, universal in its appeal.

Alternative interpretations of this tale are explored by Alexey Ulko in his introduction, with references to both politics and contemporary literature, and the author's epilogue further reiterates its philosophical dimension.

The Kashmir Song is a timeless tale, which true to the tradition of classical folklore, can be enjoyed on a number of levels by readers of all ages.

COMING SOON!!!
ISBN: 978-0-9930444-2-7
RRP: £29.50

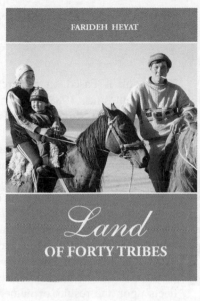

Land of forty tribes
by Farideh Heyat, 2015

Sima Omid, a British-Iranian anthropologist in search of her Turkic roots, takes on a university teaching post in Kyrgyzstan. It is the year following 9/11, when the US is asserting its influence in the region. Disillusioned with her long-standing relationship, Sima is looking for a new man in her life. But the foreign men she meets are mostly involved in relationships with local women half their age, and the Central Asian men she finds highly male chauvinist and aggressive towards women.

PAPERBACK
ISBN: **978-0-9930444-4-1**
RRP: **£14.95**

Terror: events, facts, evidence.
by Eldar Samadov, 2015

This book is based on research carried out since 1988 on territorial claims of Armenia against Azerbaijan, which led to the escalation of the conflict over Nagorno-Karabakh. This escalation included acts of terror by Armanian terrorist and other armed gangs not only in areas where intensive armed confrontations took place but also away from the fighting zones. This book, not for the first time, reflects upon the results of numerous acts of premeditated murder, robbery, armed attack and other crimes through collected material related to criminal cases which have been opened at various stages following such crimes. The book is meant for political scientists, historians, lawyers, diplomats and a broader audience.

PAPERBACK
ISBN: **978-1-910886-00-7**
RRP: **£9.99**
AVAILABLE ON **KINDLE**

THE PLIGHT OF A POSTMODERN HUNTER
EDITED BY DAVID PARRY

CHINGIZ AITMATOV
MUKHTAR SHAKHANOV

THE PLIGHT OF A POSTMODERN HUNTER
Chlngiz Aitmatov.
Mukhtar Shakhanov
(2015)

"Delusion of civilization" by M. Shakhanov is an epochal poem, rich in prudence and nobility – as is his foremother steppe. It is the voice of the Earth, which raised itself in defense of the human soul. This is a new genre of spiritual ecology. As such, this book is written from the heart of a former tractor driver, who knows all the "scars and wrinkles" of the soil - its thirst for human intimacy. This book is also authored from the perspective of an outstanding intellectual whose love for national traditions has grown as universal as our common great motherland.

I dare say, this book is a spiritual instrument of patriotism for all humankind. Hence, there is something gentle, kind, and sad, about the old swan-song of Mukhtar's brave ancestors. Those who for six months fought to the death to protect Grand Otrar - famous worldwide for its philosophers and rich library, from the hordes of Genghis Khan.

COMING SOON
LANGUAGES ENG
HARDBACK
ISBN: **978-1-910886-11-3**

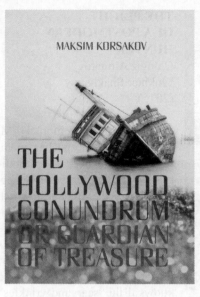

The Hollywood Conundrum or Guardian of Treasure
Maksim Korsakov
(2015)

In this groundbreaking experimental novella, Maxim Korsakov breaks all the preconceived rules of genre and literary convention to deliver a work rich in humour, style, and fantasy. Starting with a so-called "biographical" account of the horrors lurking beneath marriages of convenience and the self-delusions necessary to maintain these relationships, he then speedily moves to a screenplay, which would put most James Bond movies to shame. As if international espionage were not enough, the author teases his readers with lost treasure maps, revived Khanates, sports car jousting, ancient aliens who possess the very secrets of immortality, and the lineal descendants of legendary Genghis Khan. All in all, an ingenious book, as well as s clear critique of traditional English narrative convention.

COMING SOON

PAPERBACK
ISBN: **978-1-910886-14-4**
RRP: **£24.95**

"The true story of immigration"
— Paul Wilson is a long-time writer on the Silk Road —

CRANES IN SPRING

TOLIBSHOHI DAVLAT

The best work in the literary competition
"Open Central Asia Book Forum and Literature Festival - 2014"

"Cranes in Spring"
by Tolibshohi Davlat
(2015)

This novel highlights a complex issue that millions of Tajiks face when becoming working migrants in Russia due to lack of opportunities at home. Fresh out of school, Saidakbar decides to go to Russia as he hopes to earn money to pay for his university tuition. His parents reluctantly let him go providing he is accompanied by his uncle, Mustakim, an experienced migrant. And so begins this tale of adventure and heartache that reflects the reality of life faced by many Central Asian migrants. Mistreatment, harassment and backstabbing join the Tajik migrants as they try to pull through in a foreign country. Davlat vividly narrates the brutality of the law enforcement officers but also draws attention to kindness and help of several ordinary people in Russia. How will Mustakim and Saidakbar's journey end? Intrigued by the story starting from the first page, one cannot put the book down until it's finished.

COMING SOON
LANGUAGES ENG / RUS
HARDBACK
ISBN: **978-1-910886-06-9**